For the sake of all that is holy, don't ever g [...]
knew this BEFORE..." Too many businesses are vulnerable to unexpected legal issues which could easily be avoided. This book will prepare you for the unexpected. Read it now.

Mike Michalowicz
Author of *Profit First*, *The Pumpkin Plan* and
The Toilet Paper Entrepreneur

Navigating Legal Landmines *is a must-read for every entrepreneur! Nothing is worse than making a costly mistake that you could have easily avoided had you only known the legal landmines that were in your path. Most small business owners work incredibly hard to earn revenue. Nancy's insights will ensure that you get to keep it!*

Sandra Yancey
CEO and Founder of
eWomenNetwork, Inc.

Nancy—loved your book. I wish I had had it prior to publishing mine. It would have prevented a lot of landmines in my career. I love your insights.

Laura Herring, Ph.D.
Founder and Chairwoman of IMPACT Group,
a global, WBE-certified career development firm,
and author of *No Fear Allowed.*

What's missing from most entrepreneur's bookshelves? An easy-to-read, practical book about business law. Why? Because until Nancy wrote Navigating Legal Landmines, *it didn't exist. This book is a must-read for entrepreneurs.*

Kym Yancey,
Co-Founder/President,
eWomenNetwork

Navigating Legal Landmines *is a MUST read for all entrepreneurs! True to Nancy's no-nonsense style, this book lays out the key landmines that all business owners need to be aware of. This book is written in a clear concise manner and provides practical insights for protecting you and your business. Definitely worth the read.*

Stephanie Chung
Executive Coach, Sales Mentor, Business Advisor
Creator of "High Ticket Selling Made Simple"

We are all too familiar with the dangers our military face from enemy mines and the consequences when they fail to discover them until it's too late. We can be thankful that we don't have to deal with those things in our own lives.

Yet, as Nancy Greene so clearly points out, any of us running a business, large or small, face a field of legal landmines that can disable or even kill our businesses and have serious impact on our personal lives.

In this new book Ms. Greene shows you how to anticipate, navigate or totally avoid these situations and, most importantly, have the professional help and documents ready to handle them when they inevitably arise.

This is a book of tremendous value to anyone in business, whether it's a start-up or one that's been around for a while. I've had the chance to get to know Nancy Greene and even mentor her a bit, and she's the real deal with the knowledge to take you through the daily business minefields.

Ken Kragen
MBA Harvard Business School
Recipient of the United Nation's Peace Medal
Organizer of We Are The World,
Hands Across America, etc.

NAVIGATING LEGAL
LANDMINES

A practical guide to business law
for real people.

Nancy D. Greene, Esquire

NAVIGATING LEGAL
LANDMINES

ISBN: 978-09909111-7-3

Cover Photo by Jin Kim
Jin Kim Studio

Cover design by Rebecca Feldbush
Buckeyegrrl-designs.com

Book Design by RuneWright, LLC
www.RuneWright.com

Published by
Falcon's Fables, LLC

Hard Cover Edition February 2017
Printed in the USA

CONTENTS

DISCLAIMER

You knew one was coming, right? After all, I am an attorney. Nothing in this book is or should be considered legal advice. Purchase of this book forms no attorney-client relationship. Consult an attorney about your situation. *We specifically disclaim any representations or warranties, express or implied, including, without limitations, any representations or warranties of merchantability or fitness or for any particular purpose.* We do not give tax or investment advice or advocate the purchase or sale of any security or investment. Always seek the assistance of a professional for tax, legal and investment advice.

INTRODUCTION

KABOOM!

Your business has just run into a legal landmine. Now the business is in free fall, and you're scrambling to save what you can.

Do you know what?

This collision could have been avoided.

You could have followed your dream and desire, not been dragged down by obstacles that could destroy everything you've worked for and everything you've ever wanted.

But how?

The stories you'll read in this book come from the lessons I've learned as a woman in business who just happens to also be an attorney. I've found, during over twenty years of experience as a business and trial lawyer, that most business owners and senior managers make the same avoidable mistakes. Over and over again, my cases fell into a certain pattern.

So, what's this pattern I noticed?

Two friends start a business without a written agreement because they trust each other. Later, disagreements arise. Now, the parties aren't so friendly, and trust is broken. If the parties can't drain the emotion from the situation (and it's very difficult), a "corporate divorce" is likely. Everyone loses everything. The business falls apart, and the owners are out looking for jobs again. There are a million reasons (to be clear, read "reasons" as "excuses") for not getting the help we need:

- The business is just "a hobby."
- We have a limited start-up budget and we'll get around to it when we have profit.
- The business might not work out, so why not wait and see before spending the money.
- We can't afford an attorney.
- We found a form online, and that's good enough.
- My partner, client or employee is my best friend, spouse, friend of a friend, etc., and I trust them.
- We'll be able to work out any problems.

These excuses aren't good enough. In fact, these excuses can be very costly.

When people use them, they are building a business with a cracked foundation. At some point that cracked foundation will crumble, and all that's been built upon it will crash to the ground. Business owners, especially in the start-up and grow phases, are worried about every penny spent. They don't realize that legal fees are more an investment in an insurance policy than a simple expense. Would you go without insurance? Of course not. But people go without legal counsel. You get long-term value from the investment in a lawyer and critical foundation documents, just like you do with an insurance policy.

Your business can avoid the disastrous pattern I see over and over again in my practice as a business lawyer and litigator. And that's why I wanted to write this book for you. I'm tired of seeing the heartbreak of business owners who've lost everything due to mistakes that could've been avoided. In this Do-It-Yourself (DIY) society, legal resources are very limited for small to mid-sized businesses. It has become my mission to demystify all that fancy legal mumbo jumbo and help businesses leverage the law. Now, don't get me wrong. No book, no matter how amazing, will prevent you from hitting every legal landmine that may be in your path.

Okay, I have a confession to make.

Yeah, I know—a lawyer making a confession; who'd have thunk it?

The idea of writing about the law for real business people, much less speaking about the law at conferences, didn't occur to me until 2013. So what changed?

In 2012, I ran headlong into a legal landmine. I nearly sank my legal career. All because I made the #1 mistake in business: I didn't get the agreement in writing because my new business partner was a friend of a friend, time was short, and fear was calling the shots. Sound familiar? Isn't that what I just told you not to do? Yup.

The lightbulb moment for me was when that verbal agreement fell apart. I had an advanced degree in not making the mistakes I'd made. I'd been advising people not to make these mistakes for *seventeen years* and litigating the fallout when my clients did. Yet I'd ignored my own advice and was now paying the price.

You don't really understand what someone else goes through until you experience something similar. With the realization that

I'd made a terrible mistake, a potentially career-ending mistake, came the humiliation, the feeling stupid, the shattering of my confidence. After all, if I couldn't make the right choices in my own life, how could I presume to advise other people facing the same obstacles?

I never saw the hit coming. Life is like that. We almost never have warning of the moments that bring us to our knees. How in the world are business owners going to see the landmines in the road to success when they don't even know the warning signs? Heck, I knew the warning signs, and the problems still snuck up on me when I should have seen them coming.

The Internet has made us a DIY society. Want to build a bookcase? There's a video or blog post on that. Want to create a fire pit? Same thing. Want to know if your runny nose is just a cold or the symptom of a new plague? Yup. Check the Internet. Want to run a business? Hold on. Before you reach for that keyboard, you need to realize that when it comes to legal information—really, any services-based information—you don't know what you don't know.

For example, you might have heard that when partnering with another business, or even considering partnering, you need a non-disclosure agreement (NDA). But as it is so often, common wisdom—get an NDA—is less than half the story. While a good NDA prevents your potential business partner from telling anyone the information you give them, this type of restriction alone won't prevent them from using the information or cutting you out of the final deal with the end client. Many times, you need a non-circumvention agreement as well as an NDA. Be honest; do you know what a non-circumvention agreement is? Did you know there was such a thing? If you don't know what you're looking for on the Interwebs, you won't find it.

The game of business is stacked in favor of the house. Here, the house is the more established business that has spent its time and money ensuring that it has the best possible armor to p rotect it against legal landmines. This too has to stop.

"Wait, wait, wait," you say. "That's easier said than done."

It is. Depending on the stage your business is in, it might take months to ferret out all the legal landmines buried in your contracts and operations. It's a drag, but don't let that overwhelm you. All journeys start with a first step. This book is designed as your first step to creating untouchable back office operations. Knowing you've done everything you can to plan for the unexpected and repel most attacks gives you the confidence to stand tall in business and realize your dream. In this book, we'll go over the main legal landmines that exist for every business and how to avoid them.

As my friend and the business coach who started me o n this particular path of my journey, Darnyelle Jervey, says, "You can't see the picture if you're the frame." In an art museum, you can't stand inches from the work and appreciate it. You have to step back. The same thing is true in business. When you're too close to it, you can't see the landmine until it's far too late and it's blown up in your face. Your business needs an outside advocate, a trusted advisor who can see what you can't. I'm ready when you are. If not me, then find someone. Don't go it alone in business. There are plenty of competent, passionate professionals who are there to help you if you just ask.

Women are less likely to ask for help and more likely to make the mistakes we're going to look at in this book than their male peers. After all, we value relationships and being liked over success. Our male counterparts choose success nearly every time.

There's a dirty truth out there that we, as a society, sweep under the rug and pretend doesn't exist. While business is hard, some people try to knock you down just because you're a woman. Every one of you has a story in which someone put landmines in your path simply because you're a woman, or know a woman this happened to. Gender discrimination hasn't stopped; it's just become more subtle. The reality is, women face different challenges as employees, executives and business owners. Women in business don't have to give up their identities to succeed. But we do have to make sure we're playing on the same field. We need to stop letting fear of being not liked or being considered a battle-axe stop us from living fully in personal life and business. We need to stop hurtling headlong into the business minefield.

I want to save business owners the heartache of watching their dreams die. I want to help you shift your mindset and protect yourself in business. I want to help you pull on your big girl panties (okay, or boxer briefs—with or without superhero emblem—if you're a man) and think like an entrepreneur. I want you to see the minefield before you hit it and know when to ask for help. I want you to see that you can be successful in business.

In this book, I'll share ways you can spot the minefield and protect your business from the most common mistakes that turn business owners like you into clients for my law practice. I'm here to empower you, so you know you have the right protection and can stand tall. (Okay, at five feet four inches, I only stand so tall, but I make the most of it. In court, opposing counsels—attorneys representing the other side—think I'm six feet tall and wearing six-inch heels). Standing tall is a matter of moving confidently in your power.

When you can't stand tall, whether it's because you've just been knocked to your knees or you're too busy, frustrated or distracted by life, I'm here to fight for you and lead you back to your source of power.

Every time I speak at conferences or networking groups, several people will approach me and say things like, "I wish I'd known you *before* ..." or "I wish I knew this *before* ..." Those comments don't surprise me. I've had hundreds of clients over my more-than-twenty-year legal career say the same thing. Sometimes they went wrong because they relied on a piece of common wisdom that turned out to be nothing but an urban myth. Most people are surprised when I tell them that disputes *between* business owners are the number one reason for the failure of businesses that could have been or were profitable. I've helped many companies survive these disputes and thrive after one owner has left the business. I've helped dozens of companies in litigation protect their confidential information from misuse by their former employees. Many of these disputes could have been avoided if the parties involved had known certain legal concepts or taken certain actions *before* problems came up.

What the conference attendees, and my clients, needed to know *before* became the tips for this book and my video series. I've helped hundreds of businesses through the legal minefield over the years. When I've worked with companies *before* the problem, I've been able to save my clients hundreds of thousands of dollars in collective litigation expenses.

Women-owned businesses are the future. Even during the recession, women were starting businesses at a rate that outpaced their male counterparts. According to the American Express Open 2016 State of Women-Owned Business Executive Report, between 2007 and 2016 the number of women-owned businesses increased by forty-five percent, compared to just a nine percent increase among all businesses. Business revenue for women-owned businesses has increased thirty-five percent in the same time period.

But sadly, most women-owned business are smaller than male-owned businesses. Most women don't go big. We don't make more than a job for ourselves because doubts about our self-worth, fear and guilt plague us. I struggle with the little voice that whispers "not good enough" every day. I worry about cheating my husband and sons out of time with me. And you know what? My boys, all three of them, are the first ones to champion what I'm doing. They have my back. Whatever your reason for not playing big, for not being all you can, *it stops now*.

Your future is two steps ahead of you. Let me help you take the first step. Once you do, you'll see all the resources and people there to help you with the second one.

You have power. Realize it. Grab it. Life's waiting for you. Are you ready?

CHAPTER 1

Desire and Drag

We may have meltdowns or breakdowns, but we don't have to stay down. Desire is a stronger force and drives us forward.

I know you don't want to read this book. After all, a law book? "Maybe when I can't sleep at night. It'll be so dry and boring that I'll drop off into a deep sleep," you think.

I wrote this book so reading it won't be torture, and you won't feel like you're in your first year of law school while you do. I wrote it so we could have a conversation about business. You might be worried that this book will be over your head. A lot of the law books for business owners are written like a first-year course. Well, that's just useless. You're too busy to wade through unnecessarily dense text. When I couldn't avoid it, I've translated the necessary legal mumbo jumbo. Some other books about business law insult your intelligence because they are too dumbed down or simplified to give you any real guidance. Although it's not possible to cover all aspects of business law in one reasonably sized book, it is possible to give you practical tips and show you some of the warning signs along your road to success. That's what I intend to do. And I hope you join me on that journey.

There are times in life when desire propels us forward, and then there are times when fear or other negatives drag us back. It's my belief that life is a blend of desire and drag and, if you are really following your desire, no drag will be strong enough to stop you for long. Life can bring us to our knees, but it's also waiting for us to say, "I'm ready!" so it can unveil the gifts it has for us. Are you ready?

Then keep reading.

Should You Get Back on the Horse?

We all get into business because we have long-term dreams. Some dreams are new and some have been cherished for years. Do you know the satisfaction of wanting something forever and then finally making it happen?

Yes. Me too.

Some people dream of luxury cars, or shopping trips to New York, or wish for another of the million ways we define success and reward ourselves for finally, finally reaching that goal.

For me that dream and its reward was Taffy.

No. Not the candy.

I'd wanted a horse since I was two years old and my mom was foolish enough to put me on one; I'm a big fan of long-term goals. I picked my high school because they had horses, and instead of gym I could take riding lessons. I mucked stalls to get money for lessons. You know what that is, right? Yup. I shoveled manure. I groomed horses at shows where I was competing so I could afford the entry fees and dreamed of being part of the American Team for the Summer Olympics. I exercised school horses, even the ones with bad attitudes, to get more riding time. I don't think I had a single stitch of clothing that didn't reek of horse. I was ecstatic.

My desire to have a horse is similar to many of your dreams, whether or not those dreams are in the business realm. We've all saved money, sacrificed and done things that pushed us far out of our comfort zones to get what we wanted, dreamed of. I mean, here I was: a scholarship kid at a very rich, very exclusive all-girls boarding school in New England, cleaning the stalls for my classmates' horses. Did they look down on me? Yup. And I could not have cared less. Well, okay, I cared a little; I was, after all, a teenaged girl. But I didn't care enough to stop working in the stables. I loved what I was doing. After all, I was around horses.

We've all had people look at us and what we're doing to live our dreams and ask, "Why in the world would you do *that*?" We all have people in our lives who seem to enjoy pointing out the hard parts of moving forward, who try to drag us back to their small vision of us. Can you think of one person in your life who's a drag on your dream? Yeah. Thought so. But here's what they don't get: Our desire, our drive, to see that dream made real is stronger than any weight they can attach to drag us down.

Yet sometimes we have trouble seeing the dream through the muck on our windshield.

The very first thing I did when I got my first job in a law firm was buy a horse.

Then the dream almost killed me.

Never engage in a head-butting contest with a horse. You will lose. Trust me.

Sometimes, in life and business, we say pursuing our dreams is "killing" us. Then we wonder if the cost is worth the joy.

Taffy was a two-year-old filly one of my best friends had trained. For four months after I got her, I was at the barn five days a week. It was one of the best times of my life. Every day I was living my dream. I had a horse. I was a lawyer doing a job I loved. And I'd just gotten engaged. I couldn't imagine life getting any better. After all, this was everything I'd ever wanted.

Two days after getting engaged, I was studying for the Maryland bar exam—the test lawyers have to pass to, well, become lawyers—and I needed a study break. So I did what I always did when I needed focus: I went to the barn.

Virginia had been hit with one of its worst winters, which included back-to-back blizzards. Over four feet of snow lay on the ground, and it was bitterly cold. Rather than letting the horses out in snow-covered fields, the barn let the horses out in the "indoor" ring. This arena only had three of its walls up.

Taffy was a bit spooky in the ring and wouldn't turn left into one corner. But after a half hour or so of walking with her, she'd settled down. I decided to try that left turn again. After all, you don't stop a lesson on a negative. You stop on a "win" regardless of how small. For me that day, the win was turning left into the scary corner. The people at the barn chose that moment to let Taffy's buddies out into the field next to us. Ever seen a horse play in snow?

They buck and rear and carry on.

Taffy decided she'd had enough. The herd was out. The herd was safety. She wasn't about to confront her fear right then. So she bolted … straight through me.

Clocking me on the left side of my chin, she relocated one tooth, removed another and shattered a third; broke my nose;

nearly ripped off my right eyelid and turned my metal glasses into a twisted mess. The only reason I didn't break my jaw or snap my neck was that I never saw the hit coming. Life's like that.

I'd been knocked silly. The accident didn't just bring me to my knees but laid me out flat on my back—sort of like Wile E. Coyote after one of his schemes goes horribly wrong.

When I came to, I knew I'd been hit in the head and it was bad. In one of those crystal-clear moments, I knew I had a choice. I could stay down and likely freeze to death before people in the closed office two barns away found me, or I could scream for help. So I screamed at the top of my lungs.

Turns out I wasn't that loud. But I was loud enough.

One of the workers was walking past the barn, heard something and saw the riderless horse in the far end of the ring. He then bellowed at the top of *his* lungs to get me help.

What do they say about riding horses?

If you fall off, you should …

That's garbage. Insanity.

When I took the Maryland bar exam three weeks later, I was still throwing up from the concussion. But I felt horrible because I hadn't gotten back in the saddle: I wasn't living up to society's expectations. I wasn't living up to the expectations I placed on myself. I wasn't even willing to walk next to my horse, much less get on her back again. And I kept thinking there must be something wrong with me. I hadn't fallen off the horse, and still I couldn't get back up on her. I didn't want to hear all the platitudes because they made me feel worse. I was dragging hard. My dream had shattered and was gone. There was no joy left.

But you know what? Sometimes not getting up right away is okay.

We entrepreneurs beat ourselves up because *our* dream isn't working on *someone else's* schedule. Sometimes we need to be still.

Sometimes we need to sit still when we stumble. There's nothing wrong with staying still until you're ready to move forward. There are times when we need to stay still, stop doing and ask for the help we need before we make things worse.

But the problem is, sometimes we stay still out of fear.

There are two forces at work in our lives. Drive and drag.

When you get knocked down—or, in my case, head-butted— that's the drag. Drag is anything that tells you that "you can't," or your dream is wrong or not worth the sacrifice. Drag is when you don't get back up because you're afraid. Don't let fear run your business or your life. It's a mistake *every* time.

Drag is also when we have the thing we love and hope for the most and something goes wrong.

After the accident I was dragging. *Hard.*

There is some truth to that saying about riding the horse: If you don't get back up after you fall or have been knocked silly, the fear of it happening again grows. That fear blocks out the sun and kills your joy. I wouldn't walk next to Taffy for months. I was afraid of the thing I wanted most.

But, you know, life dangles our dream in front of us. It's the carrot in front of the horse. We have to decide whether to grab that dream. For me, that moment came on a perfect summer's day five months after my doctor said it was okay to ride again.

For a while after my injury, Karin, my riding instructor and good friend, made me come out to my scheduled lessons dressed to ride. But she didn't let me ride. Instead, she exercised the horse or taught someone else a lesson on *my horse*.

One day, we were in a small riding ring, and I was watching Karin put Taffy through her paces for the thousandth time. The day was perfect: warm with no humidity, which is a rarity in August in Virginia. There was a light breeze and the kind of white puffy clouds that you'd think came from a movie studio.

On this day, something was different. The frustration of not being able to ride my horse was too much. It ate at me. The need to be there, to recapture my dream, was too much. I wanted to feel that joy again. The desire, the *drive* was suddenly much bigger than the fear dragging me down.

Karin had dangled a carrot in front of me, the one carrot I so desperately wanted. I learned in that moment that the dream, my dream, wasn't dead. The dream had been injured, but it had healed.

I snapped at Karin that I was getting on my horse and there wasn't a damn thing she could to do stop me. And do you know what she did?

She smiled.

See, that's what she was waiting for. She was waiting for me to say, "Yes. I'm ready to take the next step." She stopped Taffy and offered me a leg up. Eight months later, Karin stood beside me as one of my bridesmaids.

To this day, getting back up on Taffy for the first time after our accident made one of the best rides—and days—of my life.

But we do that in life. Don't we? We know what we want but we don't go get it because we're afraid we're going to fall. That fear takes on a life of its own. We wait to go after what we want, what we know is right. We've all done it. I waited too long to ride. We've waited too long to share our gifts. You waited too long to start your business or to seek the advice you need. We wait because we convince ourselves that the drive that's pushing us forward isn't as great as the drag.

What I learned on that perfect summer day, when I was finally in unity with my dream, was that life is waiting for us to say yes to our dreams and joy.

Okay, I know what you're thinking. What does a story about a horse have to do with a business law book?

Life knocked me silly while I was living my dream. Life knocks us all down at some time. But life is also waiting for you to share your gift, and it's okay to ask for the help you need along the way. In fact, it's required.

Drag and Drive Exist in Every Story — Which Will You Let Win?

It's a common enough story. Three college friends started a computer services business together. Raj was the marketing genius and public face of the company, while Maria was the programmer and Bob was in charge of finances. They were going to live their dream.

As is true for most start-up business owners, they drove straight forward as fast as they could. They didn't have a written agreement setting out how the business would operate or what would happen if one of them died. They planned to formalize their agreements once the business was up and running. The business flourished. They wanted to meet with an attorney and get their corporate house in order, but they were just so busy. While "see lawyer" stayed on the to-do list, the task kept getting put off. After all, drive was in control, and life was good.

Sound familiar?

Most small to mid-sized businesses face this very problem. The owners plan to install the proper infrastructure someday. After all, there's plenty of time, right?

But then time runs out. And the company hits a legal landmine. Now drag is in control, and fear is calling the shots.

Bob was murdered by his live-in boyfriend. Bob's sexual orientation had been an open secret. Everyone knew, but his family refused to accept this fundamental truth about who Bob was.

Once they recovered enough from the shock of Bob's murder, Raj and Maria hired a bookkeeper to take over Bob's duties. The bookkeeper revealed that the business had hit another landmine long before Bob's death. Unbeknownst to Raj and Maria, Bob had been paying personal expenses, including items related to his mother's medical care, with the company's money. Bob wasn't there to defend himself, so he might have intended to apply those expenses against his profit distribution at the end of the year—or not. We'll never know. Regardless, Bob owed the company several hundred thousand dollars.

Bob's sister, Janet, was appointed his executor. The executor is the person who winds up the affairs of the deceased, pays bills and distributes whatever is left to the heirs. Janet was also Bob's sole heir and inherited his thirty-three percent interest in the company. Raj and Maria were left with a nonworking partner who only cared about how much her share of the company was worth and when could she get that money, thank you very much. The company had a hit a major drag, one that threatened its very existence.

Raj and Maria had no way to force Janet out of the business because there was no buy-sell agreement in place. Not only was

Janet reeling from her brother's death and in denial about his sexual orientation, but now the company had to tell her that Bob's share was worthless; in fact, he owed significant funds to the company because he'd used company funds for personal expenses.

Janet refused to believe her brother could engage in any misconduct. The company could sue and recover a judgment against Bob's estate (the property he had on his death), but it would still have a nonworking, and now furious, business owner. The company's goal was to acquire Bob's stock and not have Janet as an owner. Janet wasn't thinking or acting like a reasonable business owner, but as what she was: a grieving sister. It was important to her that nothing besmirch her brother's memory. Despite all the proof the company had that Bob paid personal expenses with company funds, Janet wouldn't believe it or accept the resulting negative value for the company.

Both sides hired lawyers. Want to talk about drag? When a negotiation or a relationship breaks down so much that the parties retreat to their separate corners to get ready for a bigger fight, you are living in drag. Any joy or drive you had gets smothered in the negative. The company set itself up for drag by not taking care of its business needs up front.

Raj and Maria ultimately resolved the dispute and bought Janet's stock. However, it was very expensive. Without a buy-sell agreement to set the price and force a sale, the company did not collect the money it was owed and paid Janet a sizable amount to repurchase the stock.

The loss? Over $400,000.

Most small businesses would not have survived hitting this landmine. Even though my client did survive, the cash drain significantly compromised its operations for years. Talk about drag. Had Raj, Maria and Janet been unable to reach an agreement to buy back the stock, it's likely the company would have ceased to exist.

The owners could have avoided the dispute that nearly dragged their dream into oblivion and killed their joy in pursuing that dream for years. A simple agreement would have prevented the business heartache and protected the company's drive.

I wrote this book to help you avoid the most common pitfalls and legal landmines in business. I want you focused on your dream and not the drag.

It's Different for Women

Business is hard. Being a woman in business is even harder. Women face different challenges because of who we are. Given a choice between being liked and being successful, most women choose to be liked. Men know this. They know that wanting to be liked, saving the relationship and being seen as nice make up our weak underbellies, and that's where they aim their first shot; heck, some men wield this knowledge like a weapon.

Last year, my opposing counsel strode into the courtroom where I, along with twenty other lawyers, waited for court to start. He waded into battle. He didn't want to let me see the changes he wanted to make to the lawsuit in advance as required by the court's rules.

"Why don't you just agree?" he asked, continuing a disagreement we'd had a few days earlier. He loomed closer. "You know the court's going to let me amend anyway."

"No, I don't." I stepped into his personal space. "I have no idea what new claims you want to bring, and some of them might unfairly prejudice my clients. I won't know until you follow the rules and show me the proposed amendment."

I wasn't being difficult just to be difficult. If I'd agreed to give him *carte blanche* as he wanted and he had added a complaint the court would have kept out, I would be setting myself up for a malpractice claim. My duty is to my client and the court and not to my opposing counsel.

"Why are you making me do this work?" he whined, trying out a petulant child's tone to see if that got more leverage than the blustering one.

"You'll have to draft the amended complaint in order to file the motion to amend with the court, so I'm not making you do extra work."

"You're being unreasonable."

"All I'm doing is asking you to follow the rules."

My opposing counsel was now clearly frustrated that I wasn't giving in. When bullying, wheedling and charm failed, he reached into his quiver for his final arrow. He straightened to his full height, nearly a foot taller than my five feet four inches.

"If you don't agree, you'll get a reputation for being a b—" Realizing what he was about to say and with the B-word dangling from his lips, he paused. After another moment, he settled on " … not being nice."

I laughed. Nice? Really? I'm a trial lawyer. Nice isn't something I'm overly worried about. But in this attorney's mind, "nice" was a substitute for another four-letter word: "weak." I wasn't going to let the remark pass.

"I'm not being bitch by insisting that you follow the rules," I said.

He was quick to point out I'd used the B-word and not him. The problem was, he had. And every one of the twenty other very silent male attorneys in the room had heard it too. If I'd backed down then, I would have had to fight every other male attorney who thought being a bully was the way to get what he wanted. I would have gotten the reputation for being "weak" and "afraid to go to court." A reputation like that is a death omen in my business.

How did it end, you ask?

He finally followed the court's rules.

Some men equate "woman" with "weak." They couldn't be more wrong. I've been a lawyer for over twenty years and you'd think I'd be beyond those types of games, but clearly I'm not. I face bully lawyers every day. I've had another male opposing counsel tell me that the only thing he didn't like about our relationship was that I continued to refuse to dismiss several of his clients from the lawsuit simply because *he* thought they should be. His message was, "You should do what I want so we can have a good relationship." That's not a good relationship.

When women in business don't cave to our male peers' demands, we get reputations for being disrespectful, unreasonable or a battle-axe or the B-word. We need to stop worrying so much about this. We need to stand strong and treat our business associates like associates and not like our best friends.

Being a "good girl" or "going along to get along" often means you fail in business. You don't have to give up your femininity or change who you are to succeed. If you aren't comfortable with standing up and standing strong in the face of emotional blackmail, hire someone who is. That's what I, or other attorneys like me, do for you. An advocate is a whole lot less expensive than the mistakes you will make otherwise. Call me what you want, but I'm going to protect my client.

I'm not saying this because I'm an attorney and that makes me better or smarter than you. Lots of people are smarter or cleverer than I am. People look at me and say, "Oh, you're a lawyer, you must really have it going on." But I wrote this book and am talking to you because I know. I've been there. I've made many of the mistakes in this book in my personal business.

In 2012, I was suddenly faced with a law firm that was coming apart at the seams—literally separating into new firms. The drag was overtaking the drive. The only other woman partner was being pushed out, ostensibly due to medical issues. I could stay with one of the new firms, but I'd only have the title of partner and would really be a glorified associate (read: minion) until I quit or retired. Or I could make a different choice. I had two weeks to decide.

Even though I'd been consistently bringing in over $300,000 in annual revenue, I was afraid I couldn't make it on my own. So, rather than start my own firm, I let fear make my choice. I rushed into a bad deal and ignored the warning signs. I made three critical mistakes—the same mistakes I regularly told my clients not to make.

So, what did I do wrong?

First mistake: We didn't have a written contract, but we negotiated by email so I was confident that if there was an issue about the terms I had a record. And we did—until there were problems. The email I was counting on was on the other company's server because its owner had opened an account for me to use while we negotiated. When I needed proof, it was gone.

Second mistake: I didn't do my research. I trusted my soon-to-be business partner because he was a friend of a friend. You ever done that? You ever taken a complete stranger at his word just because there's a connection, a relationship or a referral from a friend? Yup. That's what I did.

Third mistake: I let fear, not a rational evaluation of what was in my best interest, make my decisions.

I quit that job a month into it. But then I allowed myself to be talked out of resigning. I made excuses for the other side's bad behavior. I didn't actually leave until I thought the problems were harming—or likely to harm—my clients. So, did you catch that? I didn't leave for me or because my new business partner was draining the joy, the desire, out of my life. I stayed for a total of seven months and let him drag me down until someone else was at risk. Sound familiar?

I was mortified and ashamed that I'd made the same mistakes I'd seen clients make for seventeen years. I'd fallen, not just on my knees, but flat on my face, as surely as if I'd been coldcocked by my horse again. That's when I realized that, as humiliating as the experience had been, and as many of these cases as I saw, it was a wonder I didn't see more clients with the same problems. After all, I had seventeen years of legal training (twenty, if you count law school). I knew better. And I still made all the wrong moves.

Making those mistakes and getting knocked silly in business had me searching for answers, reviewing my cases over the years. I noticed a pattern. Women were more likely to make certain fundamental business mistakes than men. My clients were making these mistakes. Owning your own business when you are a woman is hard. We're terrible about asking for help. We're terrible about making sure we're protected. We overvalue making everyone else happy at the cost of our own happiness.

This needs to stop now. This book is designed to give you some of the answers to the most common problems businesses encounter. Armed with that knowledge, you'll know when you need to ask for help.

• •

In this book, I write about some of the biggest and most common legal landmines. How will this book help you? It will do two things.

First, this book will empower you. I'll educate you on the issues, the landmines that regularly come up in business, so you know when to seek help. I'll show you how to get your back-office operations right so you know you're wearing a flak jacket that can repel attacks. You can walk in confidence when you know your assets are protected.

Second, this book will give you tips on how to avoid those landmines. Let's not go out into the business world unprepared.

We all deserve those perfect rides, those perfect moments of joy. And I'll help you find them if you let me. This book will give you the tools you need to ensure that no one, man or woman, pats you on the head and discounts you and your business. I'm going to give you the tools to walk in the marketplace with confidence and *know* when you need to ask for help. Are you good with that?

Great.

Let's go.

CHAPTER 2

LANDMINE 1: Mistakes Made When Starting Your Business While Working for Someone Else

You can run headlong into a legal landmine if you aren't careful of your duties to your current employer.

Y ou've spent years working on someone else's dream. Now it's time to live for yours. The research is done. You know your next and best direction. Most people barrel on and start their new business while working for someone else. But slow down.

You might run headlong into a legal landmine.

Samuel Goldwyn, the legendary movie producer, was famous for his quips. In talking about employees, he said, "I'll take fifty percent efficiency to get one hundred percent loyalty." What does this quote have to do with the law?

Loyalty.

Mr. Goldwyn was right to prize loyalty so highly. Employees owe a duty of loyalty to their employers.

It used to be that employees understood this duty. My grandfather worked for one company all his life and retired from it *twice*. What can I say? He really loved what he did.

But most people don't work for one company their entire career and retire with a pension. Even if we wanted to, those kinds of jobs are mostly gone. Today, we prize our mobility. On top of that, most employers aren't that stable. Since 2005, most companies have cut their workforce to survive through the economic downturn. And so, many people don't feel any particular loyalty toward their employers.

But employees often forget that, in the right case, their loyalty can be enforced by a court.

Employees owe their employers a duty of loyalty. Don't get tricked because I used the word "employee." Regardless of the relationship—employee, agent, officer, director or independent contractor—when someone pays you to do a task, what I'm talking about applies to you. For simplicity's sake, I use "employee," even though the duty of loyalty applies more broadly. The law limits what you can do in starting your new business when working for someone else. You're less likely to run into problems if your new business is unrelated to your current position. But, if you're planning to compete with your current employer, beware.

"Wait!" you say. "What do you mean by beware? I don't have a non-competition agreement, so I can do whatever I want, right?"

Let's step back for a second. A non-competition agreement prevents an employee from engaging in certain activities while employed and for a period of time afterward. The company's rationale behind these agreements is: "I've spent time and energy teaching my employee my business and I'll be darned if he can quit and steal my business." These agreements generally prevent any of or all of three types of actions: working for the employer's customers, hiring the employer's employees or contractors, and offering competitive services or goods in the same geographic area as the employer.

Even if you've never signed a non-competition agreement, you will not be able to do those things while you are still employed.

The duty of loyalty has major implications for you if want to open your own business when working for someone else.

What is the Duty of Loyalty?

The duty of loyalty arises out of the common law (the law made by courts rather than a legislative body like the Senate or Congress) regarding the master-servant relationship, or whenever someone acts as an "agent" for someone else. The employee must act solely for the benefit of her employer in all matters connected with her employment.

What's that mean?

Since at least Biblical times, we've heard the phrase "No man can serve two masters." Essentially, this quote embodies the duty of loyalty in its most basic form.

The employee must give loyal, diligent and faithful service to his employer even when no written agreement exists between them. An employee must act with the utmost good faith in the furtherance and advancement of the employer's interests. An employee can't benefit at her employer's expense. While this sounds like a simple concept, it's complicated and more prone to litigation than you might think. Besides the common law, certain statutory laws also prevent an employee from benefitting at his employer's expense.

What Can an Employee Do Without Violating the Duty of Loyalty?

An employee can take preliminary steps to start her business while still employed. Preliminary steps can include forming a new company and even securing a lease if the employee isn't on her employer's time when she does these things. Essentially, an employee can do just about everything she needs to do to set up her new company, but can't start operations or look for work.

So, when does an employee cross from preliminary steps to walking in a minefield?

What Does an Employee Do to Violate the Duty of Loyalty?

The second an employee puts his interests in front of his employer's, that employee violates his duty of loyalty.

Unfortunately, many companies have fallen prey to disloyal employees over the last two decades. In one Virginia case, critical company employees approached a competitor and asked if it wanted to acquire the entire division of the employees' current employer. Not surprisingly, the competitor said yes. The employees crossed the line between preliminary steps and disloyalty.

Once the competitor agreed to defend and "indemnify" (legal mumbo jumbo for "protect from legal fees and damage claims") the employees if the old company sued, the secret meetings started. The employees made a list of which other company employees to approach and when to approach each of them based on whether they thought that person might "blab." They orchestrated a mass resignation designed to cripple their current employer. They moved copies of the company's trade secrets and confidential information to client sites so the information would be available to the competitor after they quit.

The employees resigned *en masse* and went to work with the competitor. The clients moved to the competitor. The old company sued. When the dust settled, the employees were found to have breached their duty of loyalty and violated the Virginia Trade Secrets Act and the new employer owed over $1.2 million dollars in damages to the old company.

In a similar case, an employee accepted a position with a competitive company. Before he resigned, he copied all of the company's information and planned to walk out of the building with it. Fortunately, the company had planned to fire him that same day. When the company went into the employee's office to change his passwords, a coworker phoned him to let him know he was about to be fired. He begged her to get his briefcase and keep it from the company. Well, she got the briefcase and turned it over to the Human Resources Department. The matter ended up in court. The now-former employee was barred from accepting his new job and using the company's information to benefit someone else. He was likely going to have to pay significant damages to his former employer. Instead of going to trial to determine how much he owed, we settled the case.

Most employees who violate their duties of loyalty aren't malicious. They often act because they feel the company is in financial crisis and they are doing what they need to do to survive. The simple truth is that, while he's still employed, an employee can't take work that his employer could perform, offer to work for his employer's client or offer employment to other employees without the company's permission.

You wouldn't believe the things employees have done. In another case, an employee tendered her resignation and gave a month's notice. After resigning, but before she left the company, she forwarded hundreds of company emails, many of which contained company financial information and other sensitive data, to many accounts at her new employer, to many personal accounts of her current coworkers, their spouses and family members, and to her personal account. A coworker who was not in on the conspiracy saw her printing and hiding company documents and reported her to the company. The company then checked its email backup files. In this business, when an employee "deleted" a document, the system saved a copy of that email to a "vault" file to ensure that no important data was lost. Can you guess what happened next? Yeah, that. The company sued her and the other employees in on the conspiracy.

Courts have found that employees violated their duties of loyalty when they:

- Diverted work from their employer to the new company or employer.

- Asked the employer's customers to give work to their new business

- Hired or tried to hire their employer's other employees or contractors.

- Planned a mass resignation.

- Took copies of customer lists.

- Took copies of the company's business plans or "secret sauce."

- Deleted the employer's information from its own systems.

- Used time paid for by the employer to support the new business.

- Used company assets, like copiers, computers, software, cars and funds, without paying for them.

- Used the company's office space for the new business without permission.

- Used an employer's confidential information, such as credit, billing or other financial information of the company or company's business records, for the benefit of the new venture.

- Used the employer's trade secrets to benefit the employee's business.

- Voted, as an executive officer, for a bonus he and others would receive when he knew he was quitting.

This list isn't exhaustive; there are other things employees can do to breach their duty of loyalty to their employers.

Did some items on that list surprise you?

Working on the Great American Novel while you're supposed to be operating the company's business breaches your duty of loyalty. Worse, since the employer paid you for the time to write the novel, or even if you used your employer's computer, the employer might have an ownership interest in the work.

Does the Duty of Loyalty End When the Employee Leaves?

An employee's duty of loyalty generally ends when the employment does. But not always. Sometimes that duty may continue after the employee quits.

What does that mean?

If a post-employment act can be traced to a pre-employment breach of the duty of loyalty and the issue goes to court, the employee will probably be prevented from obtaining the benefit of the breach after he leaves. In a criminal law context, this concept is called "fruit of the poisonous tree," which means that law enforcement can't benefit from evidence it discovered through unlawful means (for example, an improper search or a coerced confession). The same idea applies to employees. The former employee can't benefit from his breach of his duty of loyalty while employed, even if the benefit occurs after he resigns.

Let me give you an example.

While employed, a CEO directed a client, who wanted a high-end custom home, away from his employer and to his new business. The CEO was fired. Then the former employer sued the CEO and his new business for breach of the duty of loyalty. Even though work on the client's house didn't start until after the CEO was fired, he was not allowed to benefit from the stolen contract and paid his former employer the profit it would have received on the contract.

How does an ex-employee end up paying his profit to his former employer? Well, the answer relates to an employer's remedies for the employee's breach of the duty of loyalty.

What Can an Employer Do About a Breach of the Duty of Loyalty?

An employer can seek several forms of relief when an employee breaches his duty to his employer, including:

- Repayment of the wages, bonuses and benefits paid to the disloyal employee.

- A money judgment equal to the damage done to the business or its lost profits.

- Imposition of a constructive trust on the funds the employee received because of the breach, which means the former employee must hold in trust all or some of the money received by his new venture for the benefit of his former employer.

- Recovery of punitive damages, which are payments imposed by the court to deter wrongful conduct and are in addition to payments covering the employer's actual losses. Some states have caps on the amounts of punitive damages that can be awarded.

- Recovery of liquidated or other statutory damages. For example, when an employee has taken her employer's trade secrets, the employer can recover triple damages. In other words, if the employee's conduct caused the employer to lose a hundred thousand dollars, the employer can recover three hundred thousand dollars!

- Recovery of legal fees and costs. Most courts follow the "American rule," by which each side to a legal dispute pays for its own attorneys and related expenses. However, in some cases the winning party can also recover these expenses. Some statutes, like the Trade Secrets Act, specifically allow for the recovery of legal fees. Outside of a specific written law, some types of claims like fraud—where the defendant lies about something important and the plaintiff believes him and suffers as a result—allow for the recovery of legal fees. Make no mistake. Litigation is very expensive. The legal fees to prove a case can sometimes be greater than the actual damages from the bad action. Employees who breach their duties of loyalty risk paying these additional expenses.

- Obtaining an injunction. Employers often have grounds in these cases to ask the court to stop the former employee from engaging in some conduct or to take affirmative action to stop the harm to the employer by, for example, returning the information they took. Under the right circumstance, an injunction can even require you to put funds in trust for your former employer's benefit until the end of the case.

What Other Claims May Exist?

When an employer sues for breach of the employee's duty of loyalty, the company is also likely to sue under several related theories. In the right cases, these additional claims can include fraud, tortious interference with contracts, violation of the Trade Secrets Act, violation of the Computer Crimes Act and conspiracy.

How Do You Avoid This Landmine?

As an employee starting a new business, there are some dos and don'ts to follow:

- Do set up your new business on your own time.
- Don't take any of your employer's documents with you when you leave the company.
- Don't delete company information off the company's system before you leave.
- Don't download the company's information.
- After giving the company a copy of any of its information on your personal systems, delete this information from those systems.
- Don't use any of the company's documents or financial information, including price lists, in your new business.
- Don't use any of the company's assets, like meeting rooms or vendor accounts, in setting up your business.
- If the company's documents were online templates, don't use the modified version from your employer;

go back to the source and start fresh with the base template.

- Don't offer competing services until after you leave.

- Don't talk to your co-workers about hiring them and don't hire them for your new company before you leave the old one.

- Don't talk to your employer's customers or vendors, even ones where you have a personal relationship, about your new venture until you've left your old position.

- Do make a clean break so that, if there is any question about a breach of your duties, you can show an unrelated source for the information. As an example: Your former employer accuses you of taking the company's customer list. However, you deleted those contacts from your personal cell phone and turned in the company phone. You can then show that either the customer contacted you—after all, nothing forced them to delete your contact information—or you received the customer information through other legitimate means like searching LinkedIn, Facebook or other social media sites.

Starting your new business is an exciting time, but there's a need for extra care when you start your business while working for someone else. If you try to take a shortcut by using the former company's documents or taking its workforce or clients, you are wandering in a minefield. The question isn't *if* your former employer will figure out what you've done, but *when* and how much your "shortcut" will cost you. I've given you some tips on ways to minimize your chances of winding up in this minefield, but no book can cover every possible scenario. Consult with an attorney to determine which steps might later be determined to have breached your duty of loyalty and exposed your new business, and you, to claims by your former employer.

CHAPTER 3

LANDMINE 2: I Agreed to What?

Anytime you don't have a clear written contract,
you make the other side's performance or
payment optional.

I need to start with a confession. I think the concept of "fake it until you make it" has done more harm than good over the years. Projecting confidence you don't feel is one thing, but pretending you understand all aspects of business is just dangerous.

A prospective client, let's call him Ishmael, called me in a panic. He was leasing space for his check-cashing business in an ethnic grocery store, and was given notice to leave within forty-eight hours. Anything left in the building after then would become the store's property. Ishmael was understandably upset. He was current on his rent and didn't understand what was happening. When Ishmael told me he had a written lease, I breathed a sigh of relief. Depending on what his lease said, I *might* be able to go to court and stop the eviction.

Ishmael arrived in my office thirty minutes later with the lease in hand. While he talked about how unfair this all was and how he stood to lose hundreds of thousands of dollars, I skimmed the lease. My stomach fell as skimming became detailed reading.

His business was a subtenant, meaning he wasn't leasing from the owner, but from another tenant. The sublease said that if the grocery store (the "Tenant") lost its lease, that store could end the sublease on forty-eight hours' notice. However, there was a technical issue with the lease termination notice Ishmael had received. The notice said nothing about the grocery store losing its lease. This was a technical defense but not a win. Why?

The grocery store was owned by the landlord. So, if we fought the notice, all we'd get would be a stay of execution while the landlord ended the grocery store's lease and properly triggered the forty-eight-hour sublease termination provision. What would be the cost of this technical defense and delaying tactic? Over thirty thousand dollars if I drafted a lawsuit and sought an injunction, an emergency order, to stop the current eviction.

I let poor Ishmael vent for about ten minutes more, and then I broke the news to him. He'd read the sublease, but didn't understand the difference between a lease and a sublease or how the termination provision could be manipulated to evict his business at any time. I couldn't in good conscience ask him to pay me a lot of money for something that would only slightly delay the inevitable, so I declined to represent him. Because of the sublease terms there was very little I could do to help Ishmael. He lost hundreds of thousands of dollars because he didn't understand the contract had him building a business on quicksand. What you don't know will harm you. Your business can only succeed if it proactively and capably handles its legal issues.

A second confession: I hate that "proactive" has become a buzzword. But the truth is that, while we wouldn't start on a cross-country journey without a roadmap and plan, most of us start our businesses without really knowing where we're headed. Planning ahead can prevent you from driving into a legal minefield.

Planning can even help you prevent a lawsuit. Petros, a computer services client, maintained other businesses' computer systems. He had been in the industry for years and understood that there were factors beyond his control which might determine whether the system would stay operational, including whether or not necessary upgrades were made when recommended. As a result of hard lessons earlier in his career, Petros's contract specifically excluded from any damages claim system downtime caused by the company's failure to upgrade as recommended or employee-loaded malware. One of his customers, Know It All, Inc., didn't want to spend the money to upgrade its servers when Petros made the recommendation. Nine months later Know It All's server finally crashed, and lots of data was lost. Know It All threated to sue Petros for negligence and breach of contract as he scrambled to get the system working again and recover as much data as possible. We wrote a strong but polite reply to the customer noting that the contract exclusion meant it didn't have a claim against Petros because Know It All had refused to upgrade the server when Petros recommended it do so. Because the contract addressed a known hazard in Petros's business, he was able to save thousands of dollars in litigation expense and possible damages when the system failed. Planning is key to survival in business.

So is understanding the native language of contracts, otherwise known as legal mumbo jumbo.

As an example, roadmaps have their own language, and it takes time and study to figure out that language. The language of engineers, we call technobabble; lawyers have legal mumbo jumbo or legalese. It's not easy. I don't know why we call it legal-ease. But a lawyer's job is to help you to understand what you've gotten yourself into and what road to take to your next destination.

Here we go.

Have a Written Contract

In the "good olde days" (I put the extra "e" on old so you'd know I'm talking about a long time ago) in America, a man's word was his bond. Yet I litigate over and over again what the parties actually agreed to do.

Making a contract seems deceptively simple. Two people agree to do something and each receives some benefit, however small. Making a contract is so simple that you'd think there shouldn't be a lot of disputes over what contracts mean. After all, everyone knows what they agreed to. But that's not the case. A contract only exists when the parties agree to all important terms or have a "meeting of the minds." So, if one person understands the contract one way and the other thinks it means something else, there's likely no contract.

Sounds weird, right? But it happens.

Travel-Co wanted to expand into charter airplane services. Travel-Co hired Air-Co, an aeronautics firm, to do a "pre-purchase inspection" on a plane and ensure it could be used as a charter. There was no written agreement. Air-Co inspected the plane and gave it a clean bill of health. Travel-Co paid for the inspection and bought the plane. Then Travel-Co sought charter certification. Except, the plane didn't pass *that* inspection. Travel-Co sued Air-Co for negligence, saying it should have spotted the problems. Even though Air-Co had inspected the plane before the purchase and issued a written report, and Travel-Co had paid for the work, the court found there was no agreement because each party meant something different by "pre-purchase inspection." Travel-Co expected a more in-depth review of the plane and its flight logs for possible problems that would prevent the plane from being certified as a charter. Air-Co, on the other hand, thought it was only performing a "flight-worthiness" inspection to confirm that the plane actually could safely fly. Travel-Co got back the money it paid for the inspection, but still owned a plane that needed very expensive repairs before it could be used as intended.

Outside of a few exceptions, a verbal agreement is technically as enforceable as a written one.

But did you see what I did there? I used the word "technically." Yup, I pulled a lawyerism on you. That's why you need to be wary of handshake agreements. People are horrible at remembering details. Sometimes greed or other motives make people lie about what they remember. And sometimes the person you disagree with isn't the person you made the deal with, because that person has left the company, been promoted or died. Having a written contract that specifies what each party is supposed to do reduces the risk of litigation and of not getting what you thought you'd agreed to.

The shakiness of handshake deals gets even worse when working with a business partner. Many of my cases fall into the same pattern. Luke and Leia go into business together. They have a history (family connection, spousal relationship, friendship) or a mutual connection (friends of a friend or members of the same church group), so there's some base level of trust. The arrangement goes smoothly for years. Then the business makes serious money, and there is or should be profit to distribute. Now, the business relationship hits a bump. Disagreements arise about what Luke should get or has taken out already, or disputes occur over control—who gets to make the big decisions. Now, Luke and Leia, who (spoiler alert, well sort of, it's been decades but still) recently learned they were actually siblings (spoiler, such as it was, over), aren't so friendly, and trust is broken. If they can't drain the emotion from the situation (and it's very difficult), a "corporate divorce" is likely.

Most small to mid-sized businesses don't survive the corporate divorce. The company and the individuals can rarely afford the time away from the business, the lost revenue, the emotional toll of litigation and the expense of the fight. Everyone comes out the loser when the problem could have been avoided—or, at least, the sharp edges blunted—if a written agreement existed.

Because the parties have no written agreement, trying to piece together years of business interactions is difficult, time-consuming and very expensive. How the parties acted over the years will probably have more weight than either side's recollection of the initial agreement's terms. What the judge ultimately decides the agreement was, based on the conduct of the two principals, might be far from what the parties thought they had agreed to.

NANCY D. GREENE, ESQUIRE

There's a simple way to avoid this heartbreak.

Get it in writing.

Every time.

With everyone.

Don't assume having a written contract prevents all litigation. It doesn't. But having a written contract makes disputes less likely and may delineate the issues, thus reducing the time, energy and money lost in a legal fight. Also, you need either a specific law (such as an anti-discrimination law) or a contract provision that makes the losing side pay your legal fees in order to get them. Having a contract that specifies that the loser pays attorney's fees may determine whether or not litigation is worth the risk.

Clarity is your friend. This is where the lawyer comes in. The best way to be clear is to have a concise written document that doesn't rely on legal mumbo jumbo and is precise in its terms. Lawyers put your agreements in writing so any outsider can understand what each side is expected to do for and get from the relationship. If litigation occurs, an outsider (whether a judge or a jury) will decide what you agreed to. Lawyers like me make you ask the tough questions you don't want to think about, such as what happens when a business partner steals from the company, or stops showing up to work or dies. And sometimes the best thing you can do in an agreement is state what you *won't* be doing.

Read the Contract

We all sign agreements we don't read. And we need to break this habit.

Every year someone complains to me that the other side violated the agreement or didn't treat them fairly when the conduct was completely allowed by the contract they signed. Remember Ishmael's check-cashing business? I couldn't do anything for him because the terms of his sublease let the grocery store treat him unfairly.

"But I didn't know" isn't a defense.

A court will assume you know what your contract says and what it means. Ignorance is not a defense. So, know what you've agreed to and also know what you haven't agreed to.

After you read your contract the first time, what should you do?

Read it again.

Seriously. Our brains are wonderful and … lazy. Our brains trick us. Most of us don't read each word in a contract. When I was in grade school, my teachers used to make me read aloud and yelled at me when I did. Why? Because I wasn't reading the text in front of me. I'd read part, guess at the next part and pick up the story again. I was skimming and filling in. We all do it.

We gloss over what's there in favor of what we *think* is there all the time. We do this so often it has its own name: the correlation effect. We see what we expect to see.

Avoiding the correlation effect is one of the most important instances where a lawyer can help you. Believe me. A meeting with your lawyer when you say, "They want me to agree to what?" is much better than the one when you say, "I agreed to *that*?"

Getting the right contract starts at your first prospective client or employee meeting. Don't accept terms you aren't comfortable with and never let someone use a word or phrase if you aren't one hundred percent sure what it means. If you don't know, the court won't either.

Understand All Contract Terms

Verbal or handshake agreements can be enforced if you prove all the terms. When a dispute arises, you will fight over what he said, or what she said, and spend money to convince a court your recall is right. Why drive over this particular landmine?

Have a written agreement whenever you can. Write the contract when you can. Use clear and concise language and terms. Ambiguity gets litigated.

Words can be legal landmines. Really. Think I'm over-reacting? I've litigated over the definitions of "unique" and "exclusive." I've litigated cases about what was meant by the phrase "organic dirt." Do you think the comma placement doesn't matter? There is a difference between a "dirt-cheap contract" and a one that's "dirt, cheap." In the first case, whatever the item is, it's being sold very inexpensively. In the second, the item sold is limited to "dirt." There's a woman in Ohio who got out of a parking ticket because of where the comma was in the law. Ambiguity, whether in definition or grammar, is the quickest ticket to litigation.

A word, provision or contract is ambiguous when it can have two or more meanings. Look in any dictionary. Most English words have more than one meaning. To paraphrase Inigo Montoya, the swordsman-for-hire from *The Princess Bride*, sometimes legalese means that a word does not mean what you think it does.

Consider this example. Once a court was asked to determine if "shall" meant "must." After a book's worth of pleadings, the court ruled that "shall" sometimes means "may" depending on context. Again, though this seems weird, the ruling makes sense based on the facts before the court at the time. The court noted that, while the law used the word "shall," the government was given a choice of options. If the police officer "shall do X or Y," then he has a choice. This choice only meant that officer could do X or Y but had no other options. "Shall" was permissive, and in context the provision read, the "Officer may do only X or Y." Once "shall" was interpreted as the permissive "may," then every "shall" in the document meant "may."

When writing your agreements, avoid ambiguity. Meeting with a lawyer at the contract drafting stage means the lawyer can change "shall" to "may" for permissive actions and use "must" for mandatory actions.

Another example of a word that might not mean what you think it does is "solicit." If your former employee can't "solicit" your customers, does the former employee violate the restriction if he puts an ad on Angie's List, Craig's List or hundreds of similar fora? After all, he's asking for sales. Has the former employee "solicited" someone who calls him and asks him to perform competing work?

The Merriam-Webster dictionary has eight definitions of the word "solicit." Dictionary.com has seven definitions. Because of the multiple meanings of "solicit," a court could rule that the term "solicit" is too ambiguous or broad to enforce, and your protection against former employees poaching your clients, which you thought was armor, might afford as much security as a wet paper towel.

Let me tell you a secret that will help when you're talking contracts: The other side probably doesn't understand the provision that confuses you either. You're not giving away your ignorance or acting stupid by asking what a contract term means.

If the other side will look down on you for asking, then you probably don't want to be in business with them anyway. I had one case where my opposing counsel, Fred, was from a very large and expensive law firm and had been practicing law twice as long as I had. We were working through a teaming contract, and I asked him what his non-circumvention provision (legalese for a contract term that prevents one side of the contract from pursuing the opportunity without using the services of the other party) meant because years of other attorneys working on the same template had turned the language into gobbledygook.

This was the language actually used:

> (1) It is hereby agreed by and between the Parties hereto, to NON-CIRCUMVENTION as to: (a) the knowledge, efforts, opportunities, and procedures that the Parties involved may learn from one another or from the principals; (b) addresses, telephone and fax numbers of sellers, buyers, customers, clients, suppliers or other providers, prospective buyers carriers or providers of insurance or others, all hereinafter referred to as CONTACTS. It is understood and agreed that such CONTACTS of each Party herein are and shall be recognized as exclusive and valuable CONTACTS and the Parties hereto will not attempt to contact, deal with, utilize or disclose or in any manner solicit the CONTACTS introduced by any of the other Parties, at any time or in any manner, without the express written consent of the Party introducing said CONTACT, as well as entering into a written Fee Agreement or other arrangement acceptable by all participants with the

> Party who first provided such CONTACT. Each of
> the undersigned hereby agree, warrant and covenant
> not to, in any way whatsoever, CIRCUMVENT or
> attempt to CIRCUMVENT the other, in any present
> or future transactions.

Did you understand that provision?

Good. 'Cause I didn't either.

So, I did what I always do when opposing counsel wants something I don't understand. I called him. Email wasn't going to work for this, but a ten-minute call can and did do wonders. The discussion went something like this.

"Hey, Fred. I was just looking at the contract you sent me in the Williams matter."

"Great. Is your client ready to sign it?"

"Ah, no. I have a question about a provision."

"I don't know why; it's our standard teaming agreement. There shouldn't be anything objectionable in it," he said, sounding a bit peeved. After all, it was a "standard" agreement. More on that in a second.

"No, no, I get that. I'm just having a bit of trouble deciphering what you're trying to say in Section 32, the non-circumvention clause."

Throat clearing comes across the line as Fred switches into condescending professor tone. "Well, it means if Company X pursues the opportunity X has to hire Company Y. Simple. The provision couldn't be clearer."

I nodded even though he couldn't see it and twirled the phone cord between my fingers. "I get that's what you meant to say, but that's not actually what it says. It seems like this protects the contact information and is a general and unlimited restriction against competition which wouldn't be enforceable. Or am I misunderstanding something?"

Silence cracked across the line.

I waited.

"Maybe we could tighten up the language a bit," Fred finally said.

We took a week to straighten the provision out. If I hadn't pushed on the language, my client, who was the less dominant party in the arrangement, might have been left out in the cold because the original provision was so confusing and overly broad that it was unenforceable. Most people aren't trying to trick or take advantage of you. If you point out that you "do not think that (word) means what you think it does," most of the time, everyone will work to clarify the term. If they refuse to clarify the agreement, you might be better off walking away.

"Shall" and "solicit" are only two of many landmine words. Meet with a lawyer and take the time to know what everyday words have special meanings in the law and how to avoid the common pitfalls that come with them.

Know the Difference Between "Boilerplate" and "Standard" Provisions

When reviewing or negotiating a contract, the other side might say, "Oh, don't worry about that provision; it's just boilerplate." Well, it might be "boilerplate," or the provision might just be "standard." There's a world of difference between these two types of clauses. According to Webster's Dictionary, "boilerplate" language is "uniform language used normally in legal documents that has a definite, unvarying meaning in the same context that denotes that the words have not been individually fashioned to address the legal issue presented." Okay, not the most helpful definition, I know. Even when lawyers try to explain something we often revert to legal mumbo jumbo.

Let me try to put that in real-people speak. A boilerplate provision does not vary from certain standardized language, regardless of the type of contract in which it appears. In most states, any ambiguity in a contract is read against the person who wrote the contract. To avoid this presumption, many contracts include the following language:

"Section 33: Joint Drafting: This Agreement is not subject to any rules of construction or presumptions in favor of or against either Party."

This is a boilerplate provision because the terms and meaning won't change whether it's used in a construction, employment, settlement or shareholders' agreement. The provision is content-neutral. "Joint drafting" is also a standard term because you'll see it in most contracts.

But beware. Standard terms aren't always boilerplate. A standard provision is one that is common in a certain *type* of contract, and its terms vary depending on the deal. It may be standard or usual to have an indemnification provision (we'll talk more about that in just a second), but these aren't boilerplate provisions. Don't let anyone trick you into thinking they are. Boilerplate provisions are generally non-controversial and not worth negotiating. Standard provisions, on the other hand, are often terms you need to carefully negotiate.

You Must Take Extra Care with Specialty Provisions

Most people are pretty good at recognizing the potential pitfalls in terms related to what they are getting out of a contract and how much they have to pay or will be paid. Sometimes, though, we're not as good at realizing the danger inherent in certain specialty provisions. I want to touch on some common, high-risk specialty clauses:

A. Indemnification Clauses

The contract provision that's least understood and most dangerous is an indemnification clause. An indemnification provision shifts certain risks from the person who would normally have them to the other party to the contract. These provisions are common in most commercial contracts and are often litigated. Indemnification clauses should be carefully negotiated.

Why?

If you're not careful, you might have to give away your right to settle a claim, pay much more than you thought or even defend the other party from a baseless claim.

A bad indemnification provision can require you to pay the other side's expenses if someone else makes a "claim" against him. The claim doesn't have to be a lawsuit or even relate to your contract. Some provisions allow the other side to settle without your permission. The risks you agree to with these provisions can outweigh the benefit to you. These provisions should be fair to both parties.

Let's go over the effect of a bad indemnification provision in a contract between Angelique Author and Publisher, regarding the sale of a short story and from Author's perspective. The proposed contract said:

> Author shall indemnify, defend and hold harmless
> Publisher and its owners and affiliates, editors,

shareholders, officers, directors, partners, associates, agents and representatives ("Indemnified Parties") any and all claims, debts, demands, suits, actions, liens, proceedings and/or prosecutions ('Claims') and any and all liabilities, losses, damages and expenses including, but not limited to, attorney's fees and court costs. Author shall give prompt notice to Publisher of any Claims. No compromise or settlement of any Claim shall be made or entered into without the prior written approval of Publisher. If a Claim is made, Publisher shall have the right to suspend payments otherwise due to Author under the terms of this Agreement as security for Author's obligations under this section. Author shall defend Indemnified Parties using counsel approved by Publisher in its sole discretion.

Why is this bad for Angelique (after all, it's great for Publisher)?

1.   There's no limitation on scope.

Under this provision, Angelique has agreed to protect Publisher and a bunch of people somewhat related to Publisher from "all claims," whether or not those claims arise from the short story Angelique sold. If Publisher's sister company (an affiliate) is sued for tax evasion, Angelique has to protect the sister company from the expense of that suit and the taxes it is found to owe. While this sounds ridiculous, it is literally what the provision means.

Angelique also has to protect Publisher from frivolous claims or claims where she's found to have done nothing wrong.

Litigation is the cost of doing business, and Publisher is in a better position to bear the risk unless Angelique has done something wrong. The scope should be tied to the purpose of the contract: Angelique's sale of a short story to Publisher and claims arising from her misconduct. There's no reason for her to pay the publisher's costs of doing business.

2. *More people are covered than should be.*

Angelique probably doesn't even know who she promised to protect. Again, if Publisher's CEO is sued for fraud, he can call on Angelique to pay his legal fees and pay any judgment against him.

3. *Notice of claims should go both ways.*

The provision that Angelique must tell Publisher if she receives a claim is reasonable. But this should go both ways. Publisher needs to tell Angelique if there's a claim she's expected to pay within a reasonable time of receiving notice.

4. *Angelique gave up her control and the right to settle.*

Even though Angelique is paying the bill, she has no right to resolve the claim unless Publisher approves. The provision ("No compromise or settlement of any Claim shall be made or entered into without the prior written approval of Publisher") is backward. Angelique should have control over any settlement since she's the one paying. The plaintiff might make an offer to settle the dispute for five thousand dollars, which Angelique is willing to pay to avoid a large legal bill. But if Publisher doesn't want to settle and wants to take a hard line "on principle," Angelique can't resolve the dispute. If you give up settlement control, which should happen only in very rare cases, ensure that the contract releases your indemnification and payment obligations if the other party rejects an offer you would accept.

5.   Publisher can stop payments to Angelique at any time.

Publisher stops royalty payments to Angelique if a "Claim" is "made." The term "made" isn't defined so, in theory, a Facebook post that says "Angelique stole my story" will stop payments to her *even if nothing else comes of it*. Whether to stop payments is left up to Publisher's discretion, and there's no trigger for when Publisher must restart the payments.

6.   Angelique gave up the right to pick her own attorney.

Not only must Angelique pay for Publisher's attorneys, but she's given up her fundamental right to be represented by counsel of her choice. Angelique might find a competent attorney who will only charge $250 an hour, but if Publisher demands she hire an attorney who charges $1500 an hour, Angelique must hire the other very expensive attorney.

7.   The risk assumed is disproportionate to the benefit to Angelique.

Angelique was paid twenty-five dollars for her story. In return, she's agreeing to take on hundreds of thousands of dollars in potential risk. The benefit of this contract (twenty-five dollars) is vastly outweighed by the risk. One way to address this disparity is to negotiate a liability cap for Angelique.

If the other side won't be reasonable about its indemnification provision, Angelique is better off not accepting the contract.

Asking the other side to protect you from certain claims because they did something wrong is fair. An indemnification provision like the one below is probably all the publisher really needs.

Author will indemnify Publisher against any losses incurred by Publisher including reasonable attorney's fees and costs, but only to the extent this loss was incurred because of Author's acts or omissions regarding the story and not due in whole or in part to the breach, negligence or misconduct of Publisher.

Don't just accept an indemnification provision. Get help to negotiate and understand these tricky provisions. If you aren't careful, you might assume more risk than you should.

B.   Non-Disparagement Clauses

Non-disparagement provisions have been popping up in settlement agreements lately. The law prevents you from defaming another person. A defamatory statement is an untrue statement of "fact" to a third party that hurts the reputati on of the person about whom the comment is made. Opinions aren't defamatory. A statement like "I think Pete's a horrible person" is unlikely to be defamatory even if Pete's reputation is harmed. Defamation can also be called libel or slander. While at one time there were technical differences between these terms, in most states libel, slander and defamation are the same. A non-disparagement provision prevents the parties to the contract from saying *anything negative* about the other person.

There are two issues with non-disparagement provisions.

First, I don't know what they mean—and I'm a lawyer. What statements cross the line? The statement "I think Pete's a horrible person" is a negative statement about him, but is it disparaging even though it's not defamatory? Do all negative statements violate the provision? Is sales talk or "puffery" actionable when it wouldn't come up in a defamation context?

Second, why give the other side more protection than the law allows? The state law on defamation is enough to protect the parties from false statements of fact. Also, because the provision is ambiguous it is an invitation to further litigation. Be careful of these provisions.

C. Releases

Another provision you'll see in a settlement agreement is a release of claims. Don't fall victim to the unintended conse-quences of these provisions. Let's look at a standard release:

> *Release:* In consideration of Company X's payment of $Y to the Plaintiffs, the Plaintiffs, for themselves and their heirs, personal representatives, officers, directors, shareholders, members, employees, agents, independent contractors, insurers, attorneys, and assigns, hereby release and forever discharge Company X and its heirs, personal representatives, officers, directors, shareholders, employees, agents, independent contractors, insurers, attorneys, and/or assigns, and their affiliated, parent and subsidiary companies, and their respective shareholders, officers, directors, employees and their respective successors, and/or assigns of and from any and all claims, damages, debts, liabilities, demands, costs, expenses, interest, suits, attorney's fees, incon-veniences or any other actions or causes of action. This is a General Release.

As the plaintiff, should you sign this?

No.

Why not?

Let me count the whys.

This release has three issues with scope.

1.   The group of people waiving their claims is too large.

Plaintiff is waiving any claims for lots of people she probably doesn't have the right to bind in the contract. Under this provision, if her attorney has an independent claim against the Released Parties, then the plaintiff has waived the attorney's claim or, if the waiver isn't upheld by the court—which is more likely—the plaintiff has breached the agreement. The people giving the release should be limited to those actually involved in the claim.

2.   Too many people benefit from the release.

Plaintiff probably doesn't know who all of the company's shareholders, employees and the like are. The problem with the number of people potentially covered by the release gets even worse when you get to the third issue.

3.   There is no limitation on what is released.

Again, while the Plaintiff may have a very limited claim subject to the settlement agreement, she's being asked to give up *all rights and claims* she has as part of the settlement.

In one case, a female employee was sexually assaulted by her supervisor. The company did the right thing and quickly settled her claim. However, she signed a release much like the one above. She then sued her former supervisor for assault. The supervisor's attorney asked the court to dismiss the claim because of the release. The plaintiff's attorney argued that this standard provision, *as a matter of practice*, only applied to and was intended to apply to the company. The court, however, was limited to the words the parties used. The former supervisor was an employee and shareholder of the company. Under express and unambiguous terms, the woman had released her claims against all company employees and shareholders. The court reluctantly dismissed her claims.

Also, releases must be carefully drafted in cases with more than one tortfeasor (person responsible for the damage) to ensure these provisions don't unintentionally release the second non-settling defendant.

Finally, the more people covered by the release, the narrower the scope should be. The result would have been the same with the release above if the female employee was also in a car accident before she signed the release and only found out after the fact that the other driver was an independent contractor of Company X.

Negotiate these provisions aggressively. Generally speaking, the simpler the release the better. A statement like "Jose releases all claims against Raj related to the Lease" is often sufficient and doesn't inadvertently release Jose's personal injury claim against Raj.

How to Avoid This Landmine

To avoid the most common contracting landmines, have a written contract and draft the contract when you can. Make sure you:

- Understand all contract terms.
    - Read the contract three times.

- o Ask for clarification if there is a provision you don't understand.

- Understand the difference between boilerplate and standard contract terms.

- Negotiate specialty provisions to prevent unintended consequences.

- Hire an attorney to help you.

Although the law has fairly loose requirements for making a contract, your business needs the best protection possible. This means using written contracts to your advantage. If you don't have key foundation agreements like shareholder's or operating agreements, offer letter templates, employment agreements and job descriptions and standard client contracts, hire a lawyer to prepare them now. If you've been asked to sign a contract someone else prepared, have a lawyer review it for you and don't sign the agreement until you understand every term and its potential repercussions. Clear and concise written contracts help your business avoid many of the most common legal landmines.

CHAPTER 4

LANDMINE 3: Not Negotiating to Your Best Advantage

You will not get what you deserve.
You will get what you negotiate.

At the end of my sophomore year in college, I wanted to stay in Virginia—rather than head home to Boston for the summer—and work at Busch Gardens. At the time, I was a theater major, so getting a job with a major theme park was a big step in the right direction for my planned career. I could leverage the position into a full-time job after college. One of my college friends would also work there so I wouldn't be alone and could split the cost of housing. The rub? My friend was male.

I'm the youngest of three children, and there's a six-year gap between my brother—the oldest—and me. Dad graduated high school and enlisted in the Coast Guard. He later used the G.I. Bill to get his college degree and become an engineer. Mom, the oldest in a family of four kids, put herself through nursing school. She eventually became the president of the local nursing association and assisted in developing workplace ergonomics standards.

They were busy people. And I was the third child. They were tired, and I was precocious and a bit of a know-it-all. Anyway, rather than let me wear them down by constant pestering, Dad decided that I had to argue the pros and cons of why I wante d to do something. And I grew up haggling at flea markets and yard sales with my very Sicilian grandmothers. Haggling was second nature to breathing.

So, on my weekly Sunday phone call from school to my folks at home, I had to present my case and convince my parents to let me stay in Virginia over the summer with a male roommate. It went something like this: "So, Mom, I just got this great job offer for the summer," I said.

"That's wonderful," Mom said. "What is it?"

"Well, you know the amusement park down here? Busch Gardens?"

"Yes," she said slowly, doubt creeping into her tone.

"Well, a friend here worked for them last year and will be working there this summer. So a group of us went down for interviews. They offered me a job in the live entertainment department running a spotlight."

Pause. "So, you'd stay in Virginia for the summer?"

"Yeah."

"Which friend?"

"James."

"Talk to your father."

My mother's voice was muffled, as if she'd put her hand over the receiver, as she called for my father. I heard a soft and urgent discussion, but not well enough to make out the words.

"What's this about your living with a guy for the summer," Dad demanded. "That will happen over my dead body."

"Dad—"

"You're coming home this summer, and that's the end of it."

"This is a really great opportunity. Do you know how hard it is to get one of these jobs?"

"My daughter isn't going to live with some man."

"Why not?"

Dad cleared his throat, the warm-up to a lecture. I had to derail his train of thought or I'd lose the argument.

"Dad, he's dating one of my best friends, and I'm dating someone else. Nothing will happen between us. It won't be any different than it would be if he was a she." (Sorry, James, but I really wanted that job. If I'd thought to say you were gay, I would have, despite all the evidence to the contrary.)

"Of course it will be."

"Anything you're worried about happening between us could already be happening, so how would sharing an apartment with him be any different?"

Silence.

I pressed on. "He's dating my best friend, and I'm practically engaged. Nothing is going to happen between James and me."

Dad blew out a breath. I smiled, knowing I'd won.

I spent that summer working at Busch Gardens with James as my apartment-mate. I had one of the best times of my life. And, no, my James and I never dated. Never even kissed.

Shakespeare was right in saying all the world's a stage, but he missed a critical point. Though we each play our part, our success depends on how well we negotiate. We negotiate every day without realizing it. Whether I buy that cute blue blouse or the red one is a negotiation with myself. Whether we go to lunch at the Thai restaurant or the pizza place is a negotiation with coworkers. Negotiation isn't a dirty word. It's a necessary part of your vocabulary. So what can you do to make the process better and more satisfying for everyone involved?

Assess the Risk and Know What You Want

This seems like an obvious rule, but people negotiate without a clear goal in mind. Then they aren't satisfied with the result. Be super clear on what you want to achieve before you start. Know both your high position, which is where you start the negotiation, and your low position, your line in the sand where, if the deal doesn't include *this*, whatever *this* is, it's not a deal you're willing to accept.

Every negotiation involves some risk. In setting your high to low settlement range, you need to assess this risk. Lawyers call this handicapping a case. I had a case of employee dishonesty where the liability was fairly clear and the resulting damage to the business was over a million dollars. The risk of not getting some sort of judgment was fairly low, but the risk of not being able to collect on that judgment was fairly high. The client had fired the employees, and their fledging business was just getting started. The client had to consider what would happen if the former employees filed bankruptcy and what it would cost to protect the judgment in a bankruptcy court. Another cost that had to be considered was the legal fees and expenses to get to trial. The client also had to weigh the benefits of a quick resolution over three years of litigation. The other side had to weigh the risks of a two million-dollar judgment against them, and the litigation expenses and whatever other factors, such as adverse publicity, were also important to them. Knowing and weighing the risks for both sides better prepares you for the negotiation.

Even though we could have gone into that negotiation demanding over a million dollars on the strength of the case, we started well under that amount because the risk of protracted litigation and the difficulty in collection were important considerations for the client. The downside was that we started close to my client's line-in-the-sand bottom number, so settlement would likely require getting creative.

Be Willing to Put the First Offer on the Table

One client was worried about entering into settlement negotiations. He wanted an offer, but didn't want to start the discussion. The client thought he'd appear weak by making the first offer. After all, if we wanted to settle, didn't that mean something was wrong with our claim? While that worry is understandable, it's often misplaced.

Professional negotiators, like lawyers, know that settlement is more about the numbers than about fault. If your company is sued for ten thousand dollars (an amount above most small claim courts' limits, so the business needs an attorney), the cost of defending the lawsuit is more than what the plaintiff wants. In this situation, a "nuisance value" or "defense costs" settlement of less than the anticipated expense to fight the case may make sense. Now, sometimes larger factors are in play, like other potential claimants with similar claims, and a defense cost offer isn't in the company's best interest—but often it will be.

There's another critical reason why making the first settlement offer has significant tactical value. The person who stakes the first position sets the tone and parameters for the negotiation. You establish the terms that are important to you, and the other side must respond to them. It's harder to introduce a brand-new term into the deal than it is to tweak an existing item of discussion.

Ask for What You Want

If you never ask for what you want, you'll never get it.

A good negotiator knows the result she wants before she starts the discussion. But it's more than that. It's is okay to be assertive. Being assertive (stating your position clearly and calmly) is required. Being assertive means letting the other side know what you want while being clear in your communications and without being a jerk.

If your "must have" number is five thousand dollars, don't be afraid to draw that line in the sand. Common wisdom used to be that, if your bottom line was five thousand dollars, then you should start the negotiation at fifteen thousand dollars. I've seen people take this approach and have it backfire because their puffed-up number was so far beyond the other side's top settlement position that discussions stalled. Be realistic when you ask for what you want. Mostly, I find that starting with a position closer to my client's end-point more often results in settlement; the process is shorter and both sides are happier with the result.

If a deal must have a particular term in it to be viable for you, *ask* for that term up front. There's no sense spending time and energy on points that aren't critical. Axel, a landlord, sued his tenant, Berta, for not paying rent, and Berta countersued, stating that Axel's conduct had effectively evicted her. By the time the case came to trial, Axel needed an occupancy statement from Berta. See, the pipes froze, and Axel knew insurance would deny the claim if the house was vacant when that happened. Getting a statement from Berta that she was living there—or at least that her lease was still in effect when the pipes broke—was important to Axel. He told Berta that he wouldn't settle his rent claim without this statement. Did it give Berta an edge in negotiating the price down? Sure. But Axel cared more about having the insurance cover his broken pipes. If Axel hadn't asked for what he wanted, the parties would've spent time on issues that didn't matter. Worse, Axel might not have gotten that critical statement.

Don't let self-doubt keep you from striving for what you want and need.

Listen to the Other Side

I am often amazed at what people call settlement "discussions." I had one case where my opposing counsel spent the entire discussion talking *at* me. He lectured me on how my position was wrong and why I should do what he wanted. Think that worked? Right, it didn't. Because he wasn't willing to listen and adjust his strategy based on the information I gave him, he failed to learn vital information and put his client on a path that lead to a large judgment against him. Most people will tell you what they need and what they consider a win if you listen to them.

Okay, you say. But how do I get them to tell me everything?

You ask the right kind of questions. There are two kinds of questions: open and closed. An open question requires the person answering to give a narrative response. A closed question calls for only a "yes" or "no" answer. Anyone with teenaged children understands the difference between the questions "Did you have a good day at school?" and "What did you do today at school?" The first question is closed. Your child answers by nodding his head, or grunting, if you're lucky. The second question requires at least a few words in response. Asking why the other side has taken a specific position will help you understand their concerns.

By asking open questions and actively listening, you can avoid unnecessary conflict and better craft a solution that works for everyone.

Know What Matters

People make mistakes in negotiations when they aren't clear on their numbers or don't know which terms are worth pushing back on. Don't pay more or charge less than you can afford. People sometimes think that if they cut their price on *this* deal, they'll build a relationship in which they can charge what they should down the road. Sometimes this happens. However, that strategy often backfires. By cutting your price to make *this* deal, you jeopardize the business and its long-term viability. Remember, if the client gets a service at ten dollars an hour, that client's going to continue to want to pay ten dollars an hour for future work. Asking for a fifteen percent increase on the next deal isn't going to create goodwill or happy feelings. Realistically, you're going to keep doing that business at a loss until those losses eat away at the company's bottom line. Companies have gone out of business using this rationale. If you can't do the deal profitably for less than fifteen dollars an hour, don't.

We accept less than we need when operating from a famine mindset rather than one of abundance. It's like the old saying about gambling: Never play cards when you're short of money. We get so desperate for a client that we'll do anything to get them, even work at a loss. We need to trust that there will be another client, another deal. An abundance mindset allows you to negotiate in confidence.

Besides making sure the money works, you need to know what terms are worth fighting about. Know what matters. As an example, a new writer can spend a lot of time and energy trying to get a larger cash advance or higher royalty payment for his book than the publisher offers. But unless you're a multi-bestselling author, royalty rates fall into certain industry-standard ranges because of the economics of the business. Most first novels cost their publishers money. The margins are thin in publishing. By fighting for more money where the publisher has little or no give in its position, the writer can create ill will. Instead of poisoning the relationship, the new writer should negotiate what's important: as an example, the rights he gives up to the story and when he gets those rights back. While a writer might get a few hundred dollars more by negotiating an advance, a term with very little give, he may also lose all rights to the story forever if he doesn't know what really matters.

Negotiate in Person

Email is a great tool in most situations. Negotiation is not one of them. A person can hide emotion in an email. An email gives the other side an opportunity to practice their argument and craft a stronger response for a relatively weak position. Negotiation is a give and take with its own rhythm. Email disrupts this rhythm. Negotiate face to face whenever possible, especially when you have the stronger position. You'll get more accomplished faster.

Don't Be Wishy-Washy

If you've told the other side that your best offer is $250, stop negotiating. Don't drop your best and final offer to $240. You lose your negotiating credibility and power when you contradict your prior position. If you can't be firm, you'll likely make a less advantageous deal.

Show the Other Side the Value of Your Position for Them

You don't "win" a negotiation unless the other side also "wins." The phrase "win-win situation'" is overused and hackneyed, but there's an underlying truth to it. If the other side doesn't have a good reason to agree, then you will not close a deal. Learn as much as you can about the other side on as many levels as you can. What may motivate the other side might be something outside the deal, like their philosophy of life or some other principle.

Remember the risk assessment and active listening I mentioned earlier? Here's where they pay off. The other side must see that they've been listened to and that they get something from the agreement. The benefit can be relief from a negative, such as resolving a case without a trial and reducing their exposure, or a positive gain, such as getting something of value. The right balance of negative relief and positive gain will depend on the negotiation. In settling a lawsuit, relief from a negative will be a large driving factor. Negotiations with a new business partner should focus on the benefits both sides receive from the deal.

Get Creative

This is the part of negotiation I love the most. The best thing about negotiations is that you can agree to terms that no court could impose. A court's job, usually, is to award the injured party money. Money is good. Don't get me wrong. But money may not always be the best answer. Sometimes positions that seem very different or too far apart to resolve can be reconciled with a bit of creativity.

Lana's employment contract gave her twelve months' severance pay if she was fired "without cause" and nothing if she was fired with "cause." As often happens when I don't write the contract, "cause" was a nebulous term. When Lana wouldn't sleep with the company's president, Terrell, Lana was fired for "cause"; the company, Gigolo Tech, called it poor performance. Lana sued for sexual harassment and breach of the contract, arguing that the "cause" was manufactured. Her line-in-the-sand position was six months' severance pay and repayment of her legal fees. During the settlement negotiations, it became obvious that Gigolo didn't want to go to trial. It didn't want to have its dirty laundry aired in a public forum because it was about to go public and couldn't afford the bad press. This gave Lana an advantage. However, it was equally apparent that Gigolo would refuse to settle her sexual harassment claim.

So, we got creative.

Lana was also a minority shareholder in Gigolo. The parties agreed to a settlement amount and apportioned the bulk of the payment to the repurchase of her stock by Gigolo. The company won because it reduced its liability and risk and had no history of settling a sexual harassment claim. Lana won because she got the money she wanted and Gigolo's records reflected that she resigned, not that she was fired.

Stay Calm

The person who *must* have the deal is the one who loses the negotiation. Just like in dating, desperation is obvious. People who are angry or upset also miss nonverbal cues that would've allowed them to negotiate a better deal. Stay calm and focus on your business objectives.

Be Ready to Walk Away

It's the oft-told car-buying story. You're interested in a car and make an offer. The salesperson says he couldn't possibly go below a much higher number. You say, "Thanks, but that's outside my budget." The salesperson now says, "Wait! Let me talk to my supervisor. What's the most you can pay?" The actual sales price ends up a lot closer to your number than to the list price. Saying no and walking away has power in a negotiation.

Sometimes, no matter how badly you want a deal, there's not one to be found. Don't accept unreasonable terms just to get a deal, since that bad deal will set the tone for all other deals with the same party. If you can't negotiate a win-win, you're often better off walking away and making a deal with someone else.

Know When to Hire Someone to Negotiate for You

If you are uncomfortable with any of the tips in this chapter or negotiation isn't something you enjoy, hire someone to do it for you. The cost of having a professional (lawyer, broker, realtor and so on) conduct the negotiation for you is negligible compared to the stress and potential financial risk of a bad deal.

How Do You Stop Negotiating like a Girl and Avoid this Landmine?

Every day at noon there is a negotiation in my office. The lawyers, four men and two women, try to decide where to go for lunch. It's the same thing almost every day. We leave the building and walk to the street corner. Once there the following discussion ensues with the dreaded question:

"Where do you want to go for lunch?"

"I don't know. Where do you want to go for lunch?"

It doesn't matter who starts the discussion but everyone is so worried about the other's feelings that no one wants to take an affirmative position. But when I suggest something someone doesn't want that day, say Thai food, that person has no problem saying, "no." This is what I mean by negotiating like a girl— doing one or more of the things I suggest you not do in this chapter. As I've mentioned above, to get the best results you need to be clear and firm about what you *want* and express that to the other side. When you negotiate like a girl, you often don't get what you want out of the deal. Use these simple tips to make negotiating more productive, rewarding and fun:

- Assess the risks (pros and cons) of the deal in advance.

- Know what you want.

- Don't be afraid to put the first offer on the table; setting out the negotiation points often strengthens rather than weakens your position.

- Ask for what you want.

- Listen to the other side; they often tell you what they want or need from the deal.

- Know what matters. Don't make a term that the other side can't give you into a deal breaker. Don't make a big fuss over small points.

- Stay calm. Angry or desperate people make mistakes. Don't let emotion get in the way of clear-headed business decisions.

- Negotiate in person. You can learn a ton of useful information from a person's body language and tone. But these tools are lost to you in email, and, to some extent, on the phone.

- Don't be wishy-washy.

- Show the other side what the value of the deal is to them.

- Don't accept a bad deal just to get one. Sometimes no deal is the best deal.

- Hiring someone to help you may be the best move you can make.

Negotiation is a part of everyday life. It's a critical, must-have skill for business and does follow some general rules. If you aren't comfortable negotiating a particular deal yourself, then invest in someone to do it for you.

CHAPTER 5

LANDMINE 4: The Corporate Divorce

Breaking up (in business) is hard to do.
Plan for this event in advance.

Untangling business disputes between owners (a corporate divorce) is often harder than an actual divorce. In a divorce, the law imposes some order on the process. Without a written agreement, you might not be able to end the business relationship with your partner without ending the business. Unfortunately, business owners don't often go to an attorney for advice and the necessary contracts. After all, they don't know if the business will work, so why spend the money?

You spend the time and money to set up the business right because of what happens when you don't.

Suppose a dispute arises between the business owners. What the dispute is about doesn't matter. I've seen businesses pulled apart because the business is doing well; the business is doing poorly; one owner thinks the relationship is no longer fair; one owner stops showing up to work; or the owners, who are also husband and wife, separate or get a divorce. The reason for the dispute can be positive or negative. At its heart, an owner dispute that blows up a business will be something the owners can't resolve between themselves. Without a written agreement, options for breaking this deadlock and keeping the business running are fairly limited.

Most states have provisions to dissolve (end) a company or disassociate (kick out) a member if certain conditions exist. State law allows for appointment of a receiver (third party) to wind up (end) the company's affairs. All these court-driven solutions end with the company no longer existing and are difficult and costly. It is much better for the livelihood of your business that your business partner and you agree on certain procedures and dispute resolution processes before problems arise.

Let's look at an example. A husband, Chin, and wife, Dara, owned a business. Chin was the majority shareholder. He also had mental health issues, which caused him to abandon his business and Dara. Dara filed for divorce. The divorce judge allowed Dara, the minority shareholder, to replace the company's board of directors and appoint a new board of her choosing. Now, there were lots of problems with this from a legal standpoint. First, as a minority shareholder Dara didn't have the authority to appoint a board of directors. Second, the company wasn't part of the divorce, so the divorce judge didn't have jurisdiction over the company, that is, he didn't have the authority to order the company do to anything.

Still, sometimes weird things happen in court, and this judge was determined to enter an order affecting the company. To save the company from the divorce court, Chin, who was undergoing treatment once again, filed the very profitable company for a Chapter 11 bankruptcy—also known as a reorganizing bankruptcy. Chin immediately fired the wife's board of directors. This story had a happy ending. Ultimately, Chin and Dara reconciled, and the business thrived. However, many businesses die when disputes between the owners occur.

You should have these three types of agreement with your business partner:

- a shareholder's or operating agreement (the type you need depends on whether the company is a corporation or a limited liability company),

- a buy-sell agreement, and

- an employment agreement with non-competition provisions.

Though I say these are three agreements, the relevant terms can, and probably should wherever possible, be included in one written contract. If you opt to make each type of agreement a separate document, be careful to ensure you don't have contra-dicting terms. Again, I find it easier to have all the important agreements in one document. Essentially, you want an agreement that sets out who handles what, how decisions get made and how you get out of the relationship if things aren't going well. The outline below gives you some of the major terms to have in any agreement between business owners.

Considerations for Shareholders' or Operating Agreements

I. Governance
   A. Election of specific people to specific positions
   B. Number and allocation of shares

    C. Day-to-day operations:

        1.   Who manages?

        2.   Who sets the corporate vision/ direction?

        3.   If there is an equal number of managers, how is a tie addressed?

    D. Requirements—majority or supermajority—to alter corporate documents

II.   Shareholder/member rights

    A. Powers

    B. Waiver of partition rights
        (legal mumbo jumbo that means the right to have property divided into individual portions for the owners)

    C. Duties

    D. Employment

        1.   Compensation and benefits

        2.   Termination

            a.   For cause

            b.   Without cause

    E. Stock issues

        1.   How additional stock is issued

            a.   Is dilution possible?

        2.   Restrictions on transfer of stock

        3.   Sale of stock

            a.   Right of first refusal

            b.   Inter-member voluntary sale

            c.   Compelled sale

                1.   Disability sales

                2.   Death sales

        3.   Termination of employment

        4.   Effect of owner's bankruptcy or divorce

        5.   Effect of creditor's enforcement against interest

    4.   Payment Terms

    5.   Contingencies affecting payments

F. Key man insurance

    (life insurance policies designed to pay the company if an owner or other key employee dies to make up for the loss of that individual in the corporate structure)

G. How to resolve differences

    1.   Meet and confer

    2.   Mediate

    3.   Arbitrate or litigate

    4.   Combination of above

H. Distributions including allocations of profit and loss

    1.   When?

    2.   Who makes the decision?

    3.   Guidelines on what may be distributed

I. Participation in other ventures

J. Duty of loyalty

K. Liability and indemnification

L. Capital contribution calls

    (legalese for when a company has the right to request loans or other funds from its owners; failure to pay a capital call can result in a loss of some percentage of ownership)

III. Restrictions on trade (where allowable)
   A. Non-competition
   B. Non-solicitation

IV. General Issues
   A. Name rights
   B. Continuation of business after an owner leaves
   C. Major decisions – procedure and definition
   D. Dissolution
      (legal mumbo jumbo for ending the company's existence)

In my experience, women are more likely to skip these critical foundation documents than men. People in general dislike conflict. Women dislike it even more. After all, most of us were raised to be the peacekeepers and to value relationships above everything else. Don't get me wrong. Valuing relationships is important, and it is one of the reasons women business owners work differently than men business owners. But we can't let the relationship be our Achilles' heel.

Women need to advocate for themselves in this critical business area. It may seem counterintuitive, but setting the ground rules for dispute resolution before there is a problem will do more to save a relationship in the middle of a crisis than not being proactive about this issue. These discussions are uncomfortable and they should be. After all, you are discussing what happens when someone dies or becomes so disabled he can't work. People shy away from thinking about these unpleasant topics. But we do our businesses a disservice if we let our natural reluctance to contemplate death prevent us from implementing these agreements. When I meet with people about writing down these rules, I mention that the reason for a corporate divorce could actually be positive: The owners may disagree about two apparently good directions for the company to move toward, or maybe one partner wishes to retire.

Foundation documents set the baseline for what everyone believes is a "fair" resolution of specific anticipatable events while everyone gets along. If the parties separate amicably, they can always agree to do more than the agreements require. In the event that the parting is less friendly, everyone knows the minimum result in advance. Having these critical foundation agreements can save not only the business if a later dispute arises but also the relationship between the owners. It's important to have these discussions with your business partner when you start the company and to document any agreements reached to avoid later landmines.

CHAPTER 6

LANDMINE 5: Poe-Tay-Toe or Poe-Tah-Toe—Employee Misclassification and Other Employee-Related Landmines

Don't let the monkeys run the circus;
establish and enforce rules for your employees.

Ariana started her consulting business because she was laid off from her job and had six months' severance pay. Between her savings and the severance pay, she thought she could build her business and replace her salary before her funds ran out. All she wanted was to create a replacement job for herself until she found another corporate position. Her plan had an unexpected "problem." The business was wildly successful. Even her former employer wanted to hire her. Ariana worked sixty- to seventy-hour weeks to keep up. Administrative tasks took up the bulk of her time and drained the joy from her day. Drag was overcoming drive. Ariana contemplated quitting the business. But there was a less dramatic solution to Ariana's success problems.

You can't grow your business unless you can scale it, which means hiring employees or contractors. Workers build your business, but come with legal landmines. Some businesses are tempted to classify workers as independent contractors or exempt from overtime to save on taxes. But when a worker is misclassified as an independent contractor when he's really an employee or is treated as exempt from overtime pay when he's entitled to it, the business risks significant liability. Essentially, the business's foundation cracks.

Before we talk about how to avoid these legal landmines, we need to debunk some misconceptions. The document you have the worker sign *does not matter*. Paying an employee on a salary basis alone *does not* make him exempt from overtime requirements. The fact that the worker asked to be an independent contractor or to get paid on a salaried versus hourly basis *does not matter*. After all, who do you think reported the company to the IRS?

Yup. Your worker. Usually after getting a large tax bill he can't pay or by filing for unemployment. Now both the IRS and your state are looking to your company to pay the taxes and penalties.

It is critical that you properly classify the people who work for your business and have the right documents in place to protect your business from its workers.

When is an Independent Contractor Really an Employee?

The IRS looks at three "areas of control" in its twenty-factor test to determine if a worker is an employee or a contractor: behavioral, financial and type of relationship. The more control the company has, the more likely it is that the worker is an employee. Behavioral factors include the instructions given to the employee, the discretion used by the employee, the extent of the employee's right to control how the results are reached and the training provided to the employee. Financial control centers on the extent to which a worker has unreimbursed business expenses and fixed costs and on the extent of the worker's investment in his own facilities or equipment. Using company equipment may make a worker an employee rather than a contractor. Financial control often boils down to whether the worker is at risk for losses and if he can make a profit. Type-of-relationship factors look at whether the company provides benefits such as paid leave, insurance or pension plans, and if restrictions exist on the worker's ability to provide similar services to others.

The IRS defines an independent contractor as:

> People such as doctors, dentists, veterinarians, lawyers, accountants, contractors, subcontractors, public stenographers, or auctioneers who are in an independent trade, business, or profession in which they offer their services to the general public are generally independent contractors. However, whether these people are independent contractors or employees depends on the facts in each case. The general rule is that an individual is an independent contractor if the payer has the right to control or direct only the result of the work and not what will be done and how it will be done. The earnings of a person who is working as

an independent contractor are subject to Self-Employment Tax.[1]

The IRS focuses on the control the employer has over the worker. A worker is not "an independent contractor if [she] perform[s] services that can be controlled by an employer (what will be done and how it will be done). This applies even if [the worker is] . . . given freedom of action. What matters is that the employer has the legal right to control the details of how the services are performed."[2]

Useful, right?

Not.

Let's make those definitions more user-friendly.

An employee only works for one company. The employee works the hours set by the company at the company's office or worksite, even if that worksite is the employee's residence, and with the company's equipment. The company pays certain benefits and taxes on employee compensation. The company withholds income tax and Social Security and Medicare tax (FICA) and is liable for matching contributions. The employee receives net wages and can qualify for worker's compensation for a workplace injury and unemployment compensation when his employment ends with the company.

An independent contractor generally provides consulting services to more than one company, sets her own hours and uses her own equipment. The only thing the company controls is the ultimate work product. How the contractor gets the work done is

---

[1] U.S. Internal Revenue Service, "Independent Contractor Defined, http://www.irs.gov/Businesses/Small-Businesses-&-Self-Employed/Independent-Contractor-Defined (accessed 2/3/17)

[2] http://www.irs.gov/Businesses/Small-Businesses-&-Self-Employed/Independent-Contractor-Defined (brackets added; parenthetical in the original).

primarily up to the worker. An independent contractor receives gross wages and handles the payment of her own taxes. The company pays no matching tax and isn't responsible for any work-related injury or unemployment. Independent contractors have the potential for profit.

One red flag that an "independent contractor" is really an employee is an agreement that limits the contractor's employment opportunities. By definition, independent contractors work for other, even competing, businesses. Independent contractors still have a duty of loyalty and can't profit from opportunities or materials that belong to their employers, but if they don't violate this duty they can work for a competitor.

It's tempting to call an employee an independent contractor to save money. But misclassifying a worker (even unintentionally) is a huge mistake in the long term. If the company filed an IRS form 1099 declaring the amounts paid for an unintentionally misclassified contractor, the company, *with no ability to recover any money from the worker*, will owe:

- federal income tax withholding of 1.5 percent of the wages,

- 20 percent of the employee's share and 100 percent of the company's share of FICA taxes,

- interest and penalties

- and unemployment compensation taxes.

If the company filed no IRS form 1099 for an unintentionally misclassified contractor, these amounts *double*, again with no ability to recover any money from the worker.

Intentionally misclassifying the worker makes the expenses even worse! There, the company, without the ability to recover any money from the worker, will owe:

- 100 percent of the federal income tax withholding,
- 100 percent of the employee's and company's share of FICA taxes,
- interest and penalties,
- unemployment taxes,
- back taxes
- and criminal and civil penalties.

Misclassifying a worker is simply not worth risking the penalties that could destroy your business and your life. When in doubt, seek professional advice from an attorney.

Federal Overtime Classification

The Fair Labor Standards Act (FLSA) is the federal law that requires payment of overtime to employees who work over forty hours in a workweek and do not qualify for one of the exemptions. But beware. State law may require payment of overtime to individuals who are exempt under the FLSA, or may require overtime when over eight hours are worked in a day. Businesses must comply with the FLSA and related state law overtime provisions. Noncompliance has grim results.

A note on the contents of this section. Books have been written on the intricacies of complying with state and federal overtime laws. This section *is not* an exhaustive review of this area of the law, and should not be relied on as your sole resource. Additionally, the discussion is limited to federal overtime law under the FLSA. *No state law issues are discussed.*

The FLSA includes an exemption to its overtime pay requirement for those employed in a bona fide executive, administrative or professional capacity; computer professionals; and creative professionals and outside sales employees. These exemptions are narrowly construed against an employer seeking to assert an exemption, and the employer must prove that an employee fits into the exemption. Further, the remedial nature of the statute requires that FLSA exemptions be limited to those positions plainly and unmistakably within the exemption's terms and spirit. Ties are resolved so the employee gets overtime pay.

To establish whether an employee is a professional employee exempt from overtime requirements, courts employ a two-part test devised by the Secretary of Labor, and set forth in the regulations promulgated by the Secretary.[3]

The first component of the two-part test is the "salary test," whereby the court determines whether the employee is paid on a salary basis. The second component is the "duties test," whereby a court determines whether the duties performed by the employee are duties typically performed by people in bone fide executive or white-collar positions.

A.   The Salary Test

NOTE: As this book was being written the Department of Labor (DOL) instituted changes to the FLSA, dramatically increasing the salary level for the overtime exemption to apply as of December 1, 2016. Approximately ten days before the new

---

[3] U.S. Department of Labor, Wage and Hour Division, Fact Sheet #17A: Exemption for Executive, Administrative, Professional, Computer & Outside Sales Employees Under the Fair Labor Sanctions Act (FLSA), https://www.dol.gov/whd/overtime/fs17a_overview.pdf (accessed 2/3/17)

law was to take effect, a court issued a countrywide ban on the law's application. Given the change in administration, it is unclear if the new rules will become effective or if the new administration will rewrite or abandon them. This section is written based on the current standards with the potential new standards listed in parentheses.

If an employee is paid on a salaried basis, he must be paid not less than $455 ($913.00) per week on a salary or fee basis. Under the test:

> Being paid on a "salary basis" means an employee regularly receives a predetermined amount of compensation each pay period on a weekly, or less frequent basis. The predetermined amount cannot be reduced because of variations in the quality or quantity of the work performed. Subject to... exceptions [in the regulations], an exempt employee must receive the full salary for any week in which the employee performs any work, regardless of the number of days or hours worked. Exempt employees need not be paid for any workweek in which they perform no work. If the employer makes deductions from an employee's predetermined salary, i.e. because of the operating requirements of the business, that employee is not paid on a "salary basis." If the employee is ready, willing and able to work,

deductions may not be made for time when work is not available.[4]

On May 18, 2016, the DOL issued new regulations related to white-collar exemptions. As noted above, this law is on hold, but if it takes effect the following changes will exist. While the duties test, discussed below, remains the same, four important changes were made to the salary requirements. The DOL justified this substantial increase to the salary test as an effort to weed out misclassified workers and curb abuse of the exemption by employers. The new salary amount is based on the fortieth percentile of the lowest income region (the Southeast). The DOL also recognizes a highly-compensated employee (HCE) exemption, by which employees paid over $100,000 in compensation annually meet a streamlined duties test. Similar to the general exemption, the DOL increased the floor for this exemption effective December 1, 2016. However, instead of setting the new salary requirement by the poorest region, the DOL used the ninetieth income percentile for the entire United States of $134,004. The DOL also allowed a certain percentage of guaranteed bonuses to satisfy the new HCE salary requirements. Finally, the new regulations will reset the salary amounts every three years to keep up with inflation.

Even if your business is in compliance with the FLSA under the existing rules, this is an area you need to monitor as it may change. You should review your existing compensation plans to ensure compliance with the guidelines as new information and guidance is issued.

---

[4] U.S. Department of Labor, Wage and Hour Division, Fact Sheet #17G: Salary Basis Requirement and the Part 541 Exemptions Under the Fair Labor Sanctions Act (FLSA), https://www.dol.gov/whd/overtime/fs17g_salary.pdf (accessed 2/3/17)

Care must be taken to avoid improper deductions from an exempt employee's salary. Improper deductions from an exempt employee's salary may "destroy" the exemption and convert the employee to a non-exempt status.

B. The Duties Test

1. *Learned Professionals*

To determine whether an employee is a "learned professional" under the duties test, the regulations provide that:

> To qualify for the learned professional exemption, an employee's primary duty must be the performance of work requiring advanced knowledge in a field of science or learning customarily acquired by a prolonged course of specialized intellectual instruction. This primary duty test includes three elements:
>
> (1) The employee must perform work requiring advanced knowledge;
>
> (2) The advanced knowledge must be in a field of science or learning; and
>
> (3) The advanced knowledge must be customarily acquired by a prolonged course of specialized intellectual instruction.[5]

The term "work requiring advanced knowledge" is defined as:

---

[5] 29 C.F.R. § 541.301(a).223

work which is predominantly intellectual in character, and which includes work requiring the consistent exercise of discretion and judgment, as distinguished from performance of routine mental, manual, mechanical or physical work. An employee who performs work requiring advanced knowledge generally uses the advanced knowledge to analyze, interpret or make deductions from varying facts or circumstances.[6]

Besides this general test for determining whether an employee qualifies as a learned professional, the some DOL regulations address specific occupations such as funeral directors, doctors, lawyers and computer professionals and similar highly educated positions.

a. Work Performed Required Advanced Knowledge

"Work requiring advanced knowledge" means work which is predominantly intellectual, and which includes work requiring the consistent exercise of discretion and judgment. Professional work is therefore distinguished from work involving routine mental, manual, mechanical or physical work. A professional employee uses advanced knowledge to analyze, interpret or make deductions from varying facts or circumstances. Advanced knowledge cannot be attained at the high school level.[7]

b. The Advanced Knowledge Pertains to a Field of Science or Learning

---

[6] 29 C.F.R. § 541.301(b)

[7] U.S. Department of Labor, Wage and Hour Division, Fact Sheet #17D: Exemption for Professional Employees Under the Fair Labor Sanctions Act (FLSA), https://www.dol.gov/whd/overtime/fs17d_professional.pdf (accessed 2/3/17)

The employee's advanced knowledge must be in a field of science or learning. Under the FLSA, a field of science or learning includes:

> various types of physical, chemical and biological sciences, pharmacy and other similar occupations that have a recognized professional status as distinguished from the mechanical arts or skilled trades where in some instances the knowledge is of a fairly advanced type, but is not in a field of science or learning.[8]

c. *The Advanced Knowledge Used by the Employee is Customarily Gained Through a Prolonged Course of Specialized Intellectual Instruction.*

Under regulations promulgated by the Secretary of Labor, the phrase "customarily acquired by a prolonged course of specialized intellectual instruction" restricts the learned professional exemption to "professions where specialized academic training is a standard prerequisite for entrance into the profession."[9] The regulations further provide that "the learned professional exemption is not available for occupations that customarily may be performed with only the general knowledge acquired by an academic degree in any field, with knowledge acquired through an apprenticeship, or with training in the performance of routine mental, manual, mechanical or physical processes."

---

[8] 29 C.F.R. 541.301(c).

[9] 29 C.F.R. § 541.301(d).

2.   Duties Test for an Executive Other than an HCE

To meet the executive exemption, a company must show that:

- The employee's primary duty must be managing the enterprise, or managing a customarily recognized department or subdivision of the enterprise;

- the employee must customarily and regularly direct the work of at least two or more other full-time employees or their equivalent; and

- the employee must have the authority to hire or fire other employees, or the employee's suggestions and recommendations as to the hiring, firing, advance-ment, promotion or any other change of status of other employees must be given particular weight. [10]

An employee's primary duty is management when that is the main function the employee performs. The employee can engage in other tasks, but management still has to be the focus of his work.

3.   Duties Test for an Exempt Administrative Employee

Many companies go wrong when trying to apply the administrative exemption. A company's receptionist is unlikely to be exempt. An administrative assistant may be exempt or not depending on his duties. For this exemption to apply:

- The employee's primary duty must be the performance of non-manual work related to the

---

[10] https://www.dol.gov/whd/overtime/fs17b_executive.pdf

management or general business operations of the employer or its customers; and

- the employee's primary duty includes the exercise of discretion and independent judgment with respect to matters of significance.

According to the DOL:

> Work "directly related to management or general business operations" includes, but is not limited to, work in functional areas such as tax; finance; accounting; budgeting; auditing; insurance; quality control; purchasing; procurement; advertising; marketing; research; safety and health; personnel management; human resources; employee benefits; labor relations; public relations; government relations; computer network, Internet and database administration; legal and regulatory compliance; and similar activities.[11]

Where companies go wrong is with the discretion and significance factors. The exercise of independent discretion means comparing and evaluating a course of conduct and deciding which one to take after considering the possibilities. "The use of discretion and independent judgment must be more than the use of skill in applying well-established techniques, procedures or specific standards described in manuals and other sources."[12] "Matters of significance" relates to how important the task is, but just because the company will sustain a loss if the

---

[11] U.S. Department of Labor, Wage and Hour Division, Fact Sheet #17D: Exemption for Administrative Employees Under the Fair Labor Sanctions Act (FLSA), https://www.dol.gov/whd/overtime/fs17c_administrative.pdf (accessed 2/3/17)
[12] Id.

job is done poorly doesn't mean the employee is exempt.[13] An administrative employee who proofs ad copy for typos and follows up with the designer about deadlines is unlikely to be exempt if she has no say in the design process or if her suggestions for design must be approved by a superior. On the other hand, an employee who can approve the design elements may be exempt as she's using independent judgment over a matter of significance, e.g. the final product.

4.   Duties Test for HCEs

HCEs have a streamlined duties test. The regulations contain a special rule for highly-compensated workers who are paid total annual compensation of $100,000 ($134,004) or more. A highly compensated employee is deemed exempt under Section 13(a)(1) if:

> 1. The employee earns total annual compensation of $100,000 ($134,004) or more, which includes at least $455 per week ($917 per week) paid on a salary basis;
>
> 2. The employee's primary duty includes performing office or non-manual work; and
>
> 3. The employee customarily and regularly performs at least one of the exempt duties or responsibilities of an exempt executive, administrative or professional employee.

An employee may qualify as an exempt highly-compensated executive if the employee customarily and regularly directs the work of two or more other employees, even though the employee

---

[13] Id.

does not meet all of the other requirements in the standard test for exemption as an executive. To make matters even more confusing, the salary and salary basis requirements do not apply to bona fide practitioners of law or medicine. These professionals are exempt if they are engaged in the practice of law or medicine no matter how much they earn.

For more general information on exemptions, please visit my website, www.AttorneyNancyGreene.com/resources.

Must-Have Employment Agreements

Employee management is difficult and time-consuming. A business needs policies and procedures to establish the company culture and proper conduct for its employees. A business also needs agreements that protect it from its workers, whether employees or independent contractors. Some of these agreements include:

A.   Job Description and Offer Letter

If you are a solo business owner, writing down what you do allows you to determine when it's time to grow your business. The business's first job description for its owner should specify everything the owner does to support the business. Then the owner can review the information to determine which tasks she could keep doing (marketing, corporate vision, those tasks she likes and those only she can do) and which she should give to her first employee or contractor.

When you have employees, job descriptions ensure that there isn't later confusion about their scope of responsibility and help you classify the position for overtime considerations. Setting out legitimate business requirements, such as a lifting requirement for a warehouse worker or unaccented English for a help desk employee, also may help the company if it is later charged with discrimination or violation of the Americans with Disabilities Act (ADA).

Similarly, the offer letter sets out the company's compensation agreement and establishes the employee's title, what pre-conditions exist on that employment and the employee's "at will" employment status, meaning that the employee can be fired with or without notice at any time for any reason and is not hired for a specific duration. As an example, before employment, a company cannot require a prospective employee to take a drug test. However, once an offer is made, successfully passing a drug test can be a condition for final approval of employment. Even if your company has a more formal agreement with the employee—for example, a full employment agreement, confidentiality agreement or non-competition agreement—the employee should receive and sign, as "accepted," an offer letter.

B.   Confidentiality Agreement

Confidentiality agreements prevent sensitive business information from being used by the wrong people. State law provides automatic protection for trade secrets (discussed in more detail in Chapter 9). While an independent contractor can't have post-employment restrictions and still be an actual independent contractor, a company and its contractors can and should have a confidentiality agreement that prevents the contractor from using the business's information to benefit another company.

C.   Independent Contractor Agreement

Because an independent contractor isn't an employee, that contractor owns what she creates for your business unless you have a written agreement conveying ownership to your company. Nadia hired a graphic artist to create an avatar/logo for her new podcast. No written agreement existed. The logo was a caricature of Nadia. A problem arose shortly after the logo was created because Barbara, the artist, claimed she owned the avatar. Worse, as an independent contractor, Barbara actually did own the work.

Generally, the person who creates a "work"—a print or electronic manuscript, a sound recording, a computer software program, or other similar concrete medium—owns it and the copyright. Only the author and people claiming through the author can claim a copyright. This book was copyrighted the moment I typed the first word, without my having to register it or take any other action.

Copyright and ownership laws can be problematic if you're hiring someone other than an employee to create a product for your business. However, the law recognizes an exception in "works for hire." Let's take the easy one first. If an employee creates the work within his period of employment, the work is considered "work for hire." The company owns the work product.

The issue gets murky when the person creating the work is an independent contractor. Work specially ordered or commissioned for use by an independent contractor is *only* deemed to be "work for hire" if the parties expressly *agree* it is "work for hire" *in writing, in advance*, and if it can be considered at least one of these:

1. a contribution to a collective work,
2. a part of a motion picture or other audiovisual work,
3. a translation,

4. a supplementary work,
5. a compilation,
6. an instructional text,
7. a test,
8. answer material for a test, or
9. an atlas.[14]

If the factors of this doctrine are met, the *employer* and not the creator is the owner of the work. Without a work for hire agreement, you may have to pay for the right to use the product created by your independent contractor, who can sell that product to other parties.

If your independent contractor isn't working on a project that falls into one of the nine categories for "work for hire" protections, then you absolutely need a contract provision that assigns the ownership and copyright for the project to your company.

Let's go back to Nadia's problem with Barbara. The logo doesn't fall into the work for hire categories. Unless there is a written agreement conveying ownership of the logo to Nadia, Barbara still owns the logo, and, at best, Nadia had a license to use the logo for a specific purpose. There was no written agreement, so Barbara kept the ownership of the logo. Nadia paid twice: once to create the design and a second time to obtain ownership of the logo.

Similar problems happen every time someone who is not an employee creates a product for you. This means contractors like your web designer. If your web designer obtained your company's domain name, do you own the name or does the web

---

[14] United States Copyright Office, "Works Made for Hire," https://www.copyright.gov/circs/circ09.pdf and Section 101 of the Copyright Act (title 17 of the U.S. Code) (accessed 2/3/17)

designer? Odds are, your web designer does. Unless you have a written agreement stating that you own the domain name, your web designer has a choke hold on your business. After all, you've created your brand around the company name and website URL. Having to pay an exorbitant amount to purchase the domain name from your former web designer or having to redirect all your business to a new website can be expensive and devastating for your business.

Another example of the way you can inadvertently stumble over this landmine is if you have someone writing copy for you. Whether your company hires a contractor to write content for your website, blog posts, podcasts or marketing materials, you need an agreement to ensure that you own the finished product. Remember, the work for hire doctrine only applies to nine limited types of work, and even then only if the agreement that the doctrine applies is in writing.

Don't stumble over this landmine. It's an easy one to avoid. Have a written agreement that secures ownership of any materials created by any independent contractor you hire.

D.   Company Policies and Procedures

An operations handbook allows your business to grow and your new employees to find the information they need to complete a task without turning to you for every answer. Once you have employees, you need certain critical employment policies to protect your business. These include an equal employment opportunity statement, a social media policy, anti-harassment and discrimination policies, prevention of violence in the workplace policy, reporting policy, confidentiality policies and disciplinary policy, to name a few. If you have a business with special safety needs, then a safety policy and handbook is a must as well.

Ending the Employer-Employee Relationship

I got a call from a client, Construction Co., the other day asking if they could fire an employee. It's an unfortunate truth that, if you have employees, at some time you will have to fire one or more of them. That call, however, was a red flag for me. Why?

In most cases, an employer may fire an employee. The fact that Construction Co. is asking if it can fire an employee tells me something more is going on. There are two types of employees: "at will," and "term" or "for cause" employees. An at will employee can be fired for any reason or no reason so long as the reason isn't an unlawful one. Okay. Not a helpful definition, I know. What this boils down to is, an at will employee can be fired at any time, even when the employer doesn't have a just cause for termination. On the other hand, term or "for cause" employment can only be ended when the time period, or term, expires or if the employee has done something wrong. That something wrong, or cause, is defined by your contract or the law. We're going to talk about ending both types of employment relationships.

Despite what you might have heard, there is no good time or day to let someone go. You're about to shove your former employee onto a path he didn't expect to walk. However, as the employer, you can do six things to make the transition easier on the employee and less likely to create liability for the company.

The first question I ask when a client wants to let someone go is, "Will the employee be surprised?" A "yes" response is a landmine moment. Surprised employees often feel unfairly treated. They get angry and are more likely to claim their firing was wrongful than people who understand why the decision was made and had a chance to fix any objectionable conduct before losing their job.

An employee should see the writing on the wall before being pulled into a termination meeting. Your company should have a written termination of employment policy that lets the employee know how and why a separation of employment can occur. Even if progressive discipline isn't required by your state or by your written policies, you'll often want to follow this procedure. Progressive discipline occurs when each violation results in an escalation of warnings and reprimands until termination of employment. Progressive discipline isn't appropriate when the employee poses a safety concern, whether that concern is for the physical welfare of workspace, equipment or people or for the company's information or reputation; or when the employee has engaged in serious conduct that can't be fixed, such as stealing from the company. Even then, the immediate response should be to put the employee on unpaid leave before pulling the termination trigger.

Companies spend a lot of money developing their employees, and mostly want to keep them. Progressive discipline often allows the company to salvage a relationship with a potentially good employee. The first time the employee's conduct falls below expectations, they should receive a gentle talking to or, in more formal terms, a verbal warning. Don't let the fact that this is a conversation fool you into thinking you don't need to write anything down. Even verbal warnings need a written statement for the employee's file. Explain very clearly why the employee's actions were a problem, the steps she needs to take in order to correct the problem, the time frame within which she has to correct the problem and what will happen if she doesn't correct it.

The next time the employee falls below standards, she should receive a written reprimand. The company should have a form for managers to use. The form must be completed before the meeting with the employee. Again, the reprimand should clearly state what the employee did wrong, how she can correct her conduct and what will happen if she fails to correct the problem. During the meeting, the manager should go over the content of the form. The employee should be asked to sign the form, acknowledging receipt of the reprimand, and be given a copy of the document. Don't worry if the employee refuses to sign. If that happens, write on her signature line the phrase "refused to sign" for the file. If the employee wants to write a response to the reprimand, let her. Review the response to see if you need to revise any decision or investigate any claims. Once any issues raised in the response are addressed, put the response in the employee's file. If the employee has raised a matter that needs further investigation, that investigation and its result should also be written up and included in the employee's file.

If the employee slips up again and you decide she is no longer a valuable team member, you can move to termination of employment. While the employee might not like your decision, she'll at least understand the basis for it.

That day, Construction Co., had called about whether they could fire an employee who tried to run over the company's president with a truck. No joke. Luckily, the president was a nimble fellow. So, why did Construction Co. call me when the actions were so bad that an immediate firing was warranted?

This takes us to the second tip: Check your company documentation before you fire.

Sometimes there's a reason to delay the firing.

The homicidal employee, we'll call him Jack, had filed a discrimination claim with the Equal Opportunities Commission (EEOC), alleging that he was given less advantageous work assignments and disciplined for being late when other people of a different ethnic group weren't. Jack couldn't be fired or otherwise retaliated against *because he filed the complaint*; but he thought that meant he couldn't be fired at all. He was wrong. Construction Co. could still fire Jack for reasons unrelated to his complaint. Review of Jack's employment file showed us that extra care had to be taken in his firing because of the complaint. Here Jack's attendance record had suffered because he didn't think he could be fired and, well, he tried to kill the company's president. So, the company fired him.

Nothing's worse than wanting to fire an employee for a cause like excessive absenteeism and then not having the documentation to support the cause. When this happens, and if the cause doesn't rise to emergency level, slow down and go through the process. An employee who is habitually late will behave for a time after a warning, but then go back to his old ways. Then you can document the tardiness.

Every time you think about firing an employee, you need to *review her file* to ensure that the termination is free from any form of discrimination and the basis for the decision is properly documented. In larger companies especially, an improper purpose such as discrimination may be at work without the human resources professional who is handling the termination knowing about it, because he doesn't directly interact with the employee. Reviewing the file and basis for the termination discussion often avoids liability for the company down the road.

If the employee is a term employee who can only be fired for cause, you must review her contract and file. The contract will specify what actions or inactions will end the employment relationship before the end of the term. The employee's or contractor's file should have sufficient documentation to support any cause of termination. If the basis for the termination isn't well documented, the business should wait until it has properly documented the cause.

Okay, so now the employee has been warned, and the company's documentation of the issues leading to the termination of employment are properly documented. It's time to have *the* discussion. Prepare in advance. Have a written termination of employment letter that informs the employee he is being let go and what steps he needs to take next regarding any carryover benefits like COBRA insurance or a 401K. Have a checklist of all the company property—keys, cell phones, computers and so on—that you will need to get back from the employee.

Have the employee's last paycheck prepared. Some states, like California, require that the employee be paid in full when fired, while others, like Virginia, only require that the last paycheck be given in the ordinary payroll cycle. Even if your state allows later payment, pay the employee for the last day and give her that final check during the meeting.

Have a company witness with you for the termination meeting. Having the meeting mid-morning before the coffee break or just before lunch is somewhat better than at other times, as the office will be quieter and this will allow the employee to collect his belongings without everyone in the office gaping.

Keep the meeting short and factual. Let the employee know she's being let go within the first five or ten minutes of the meeting. There's no reason to drag the process on. Answer the employee's questions, but don't get into a debate with her. Don't offer advice or assign blame. Unless there is a significant security risk, allow the employee to gather her things and don't escort her out of the office as if she was a criminal. Maintaining the employee's dignity costs you nothing and could save you from a lawsuit.

Secure the company's property. During the meeting, you need to obtain the company's physical property: keys, phones and so on. While the employee is in the meeting, the IT department should change the employee's password and lock him out of sensitive systems. If the employee has personal information on the company computer system, he should work with the IT department (or person) to obtain a copy of the information and remove it from the company computers. Contacts belong to the company. Have the locks or security codes changed at close of business so you don't interrupt the workday but also ensure that the employee can't cause mischief that evening. Even a seemingly mild-mannered individual can act poorly when upset. It's better to be safe and plan for mischief than to find out later that you were wrong about the former employee's response to the firing.

Obtain a release of claims. The best way to avoid litigation is to obtain a release of claims so the employee can't sue. Offer your former employee a severance payment in return for a release of all claims, even when the company has done nothing wrong. A few weeks' pay is a small price to pay to avoid tens of thousands of dollars in litigation costs. If there is a potential for company liability, you have an opportunity to settle the claim early and to everyone's advantage. Realize that if there is a potential for a viable claim, your severance or settlement payment must reflect the risk to the company from that claim. The greater the potential risk, the larger the severance payment. If your employee has company property at home, the severance payment should also be contingent on getting that property back.

Don't contest unemployment unless it's clear the company has a strong basis to do so. Finally, most fired employees are entitled to unemployment compensation unless they've done something terribly wrong. States have varied rules, but in Virginia, for example, an employer must show willful misconduct by the employee to have benefits denied. If you don't have very strong documentary evidence of misconduct, you are unlikely to win the benefits challenge. By contesting benefits when you don't have a strong case, you may anger your former employee to the point where she will file suit rather than let a perceived slight or claim pass by.

How to Avoid Firing Landmines

While there is no good time to fire an employee, you can take a few steps to minimize the risk of later claims by that employee. To review, these are:

- When appropriate, use progressive discipline to notify the employee of any issues and give her a chance to correct these problems before firing.

- Always review the employee's file before making a termination decision to ensure performance issues were properly documented, to be sure there is a legitimate non-discriminatory basis for the termination decision and to ascertain if any caution flags, such as a pending discrimination claim, exist.

- Prepare for the termination meeting, don't go in alone and treat the employee with respect and leave her dignity intact.

- Take all necessary and reasonable steps to recover and safeguard the company's property.

- Offer a reasonable settlement payment in return for a release of claims.

- Don't fight the employee's unemployment compensation unless his conduct was egregious.

Employees are the lifeblood of your business. To avoid the legal landmines that come with them, a business must properly document business relationships, properly classify its workers as independent contractors or employees, determine which employees are owed overtime, document the policies and procedures the employee will be expected to uphold and perform, protect its corporate information and document any performance issues. The process of employee management can be overwhelming. Seek advice from competent professionals. The cost of their assistance is far less than letting an employee-related landmine blow up your business.

CHAPTER 7

LANDMINE 6: Mismanaging the Client Relationship

Clear communications and documents make
clients into raving fans.

Y ou've set up your business, marketed the heck out of it
and now you have your first client—or your five
hundredth.

Congratulations!

Jose set up his freelance editing company. He gave clients, both published and unpublished writers, estimates for his editing services based on the quality of the first three chapters of the book and the total word count. A previously published writer, Victor, requested a quote from Jose. Based on the first three chapters, Jose estimated that he'd spend twenty hours on the project and gave Victor an estimate. Jose's email contained a note that the figure was an estimate only and the actual cost might be more or less depending on the quality of the rest of the manuscript; authors work hard on their first three chapters since agents usually request them when considering whether to represent a book.

Jose soon discovered that the rest of the manuscript was in a first draft stage rather than the polished prose of the first three chapters. Editing the novel would take much more than twenty hours. Jose submitted a revised estimate. Victor went through the roof and accused Jose of bait and switch tactics. He reported Jose to an unofficial writers' oversight board, Science Fiction & Fantasy Writers of America (SFWA), and an influential writers' forum, Predators & Editors. Jose's career as an editor and membership in SFWA was at risk. Jose could have easily avoided this legal landmine by properly managing the client relationship.

Clients come with their own legal landmines. Some potential problem areas are inherent in any business and customer relationship regardless of the industry. Additional issues arise when your business works directly with consumers who are purchasing for primarily personal, household or family reasons. Consumers receive extra protection under the law. If you aren't careful, your business can make payment optional for its customers.

Have a Written Contract

The first mistake a business can make working with clients is not having a written agreement. I wrote in detail about the value of a written contract in Chapter 2. Take a second to review that chapter. Back? Great. Let's build on that foundation then.

A contract sets the parties' expectations and is a business's best tool to manage its client relationships. Business owners worry about clients not signing their agreement. So, rather than take the risk of not getting the work, the business starts without a contract. Please, don't make this mistake. Don't let fear keep your business from getting the protection it deserves.

Contracts don't have to be dozens of pages long. The contract must simply be long enough cover all the "material" terms (legal mumbo jumbo for "important" items). Ideally, the business has a short, clear agreement with standard terms and conditions. Making a new contract for every client becomes an administrative nightmare and increases the risk that some detail will be lost in a special arrangement.

When a business offers different services, it might need different contracts for those services. As an example, my speaker contract differs from my consulting contract, and I have several legal services contracts that I use for different representation and billing arrangements. However, all my contracts are standardized, meaning each client for that service has the same terms and conditions.

A client services contract should cover:

A.   Scope of work

Be specific about what the business will and won't do. As an example, in bankruptcy courts the lawyer for the debtor (the person filing bankruptcy) has to disclose to the court what the lawyer has been paid and what she has agreed to do for the payment. It's not uncommon to see terms scratched out from the court's standard form and others added to show what the lawyer will and won't do for her fee. More businesses need to take this approach to contracting. This way, you know what your product or the end result will look like. It is probably in your best interest to specify what will be delivered to the client. Many businesses fear doing this because they think being specific makes litigation more likely. In fact, the opposite is true. Being specific helps everyone involved in the transaction understand what to expect, and when you over-deliver (because we know you will), you can easily show where you went above and beyond. Also, it's sometimes more important for a business to specify what it will not do than what it will do.

Marko, a business owner was operating two businesses, Old-Co and New-Co, under one QuickBooks account. He hired an independent contractor and bookkeeper, Deva, to separate the businesses' finances, and she agreed to a fee for that work plus a year of bookkeeping for both companies. The records were in worse shape than Deva was led to believe, but she didn't tell Marko or ask for a price adjustment because she was happy about the twelve-month contract. Separating the records took longer than originally planned. Deva extracted the information for New-Co into its own QuickBooks account, but left New-Co's information in Old-Co's records, properly flagged as New-Co's expenses. Marko wasn't pleased. He'd expected to have all of New-Co's records purged from Old-Co's files. He refused to pay and canceled the twelve months' services contract. Deva was upset that she had over-delivered without compensation, and Marko was upset that he didn't get what he assumed he would. The parties ended up in litigation because they weren't clear on what the final product would look like. In the long run, even though the case settled, both sides lost.

If certain services might be considered within the scope of the work, but you intend to exclude them because the client doesn't want or can't afford them, specifically carve these services out of the agreement.

B. Compensation terms

Client payments should not be optional. Contracts should clearly explain how the business will charge for its services, whether on an hourly, flat rate or some other basis. They should also make clear when payments are due, and any other important payment terms.

Jose could have avoided the dispute with Victor over the editing costs, or at least minimized the likely repercussions, with a written contract which clearly stated that Jose's quote was merely an estimate; how any changes to the price would be calculated; how and when Victor would be notified of the price change; and an option for Victor to decline the additional work and pay only for the work completed at the time of notice. Instead of being paid a reasonable rate for his work and having a happy customer, Jose edited the novel for free to save his professional reputation.

C. Term

The term is the length of the contract. Some contracts are for a specific duration rather than a specific task. If so, make sure the term is clearly set out.

D. Default terms

A "default" is when a party fails to perform an obligation under the agreement. A default is "material" and grounds for a breach of contract claim when failing to fulfil the obligation goes to the heart of the agreement—such as when the client fails to pay. There should be repercussions for a default. Consequences can include termination of the contract, late fees, a higher rate of interest on the balance due, legal fees and other relief.

E.   Basis to end the contract, or an out clause

A lot of contracts don't have an "out" or a way to end services if something goes wrong or the relationship isn't working. Don't get stuck performing services for a client you no longer wish to work with. Have a way out of the relationship, especially one that may last for years. When you cringe every time a certain client calls or when he won't call back and you want to tear your hair out, it's time to end the relationship. An out clause will allow you to terminate the agreement for conduct or issues that don't actually violate the agreement but make working with the client a chore.

Take the example above, Deva had a twelve-month contract—but what happens if Marko stops giving her the information she needs to perform? How is she supposed to meet her production deadlines? Rather than deal with a later fight about who violated the agreement, Deva could have a provision in her contract that lets her stop services if Marko fails to provide the required information within a specific time period and still collect on the balance of her contract. She has an "out" clause that way. Anytime you're entering into a long-term contract, you want terms that allow you to stop and end the agreement if the relationship or financial structure of the deal no longer works for you.

F.   Governing law and jurisdiction

A contract is generally governed by the last place it's signed. When your client is based in another state, you might find yourself covered by laws you didn't intend to be covered by. To avoid this result, your contract should state that it is governed by the laws of your state, not the client's, and that all litigation occurs where your business is located.

G.   Limitations on liability, if appropriate

In certain cases, you will want to limit the claims and the damages from those claims that can arise from the contract's performance. Remember the example in Chapter 3 where Petros's IT service company disclaimed liability for website crashes caused by someone hacking the site or by a client employee, accidently or intentionally, loading malware onto the system? The limitation in liability in Petros's contract saved him a bundle. Similarly, home inspectors often limit their liability for anything they missed in the inspection to the amount the homeowner paid for the inspection. Some limits on liability won't be enforced, such as a release of negligence claims in some states. If your business will use a damages or liability limitation provision, consult with an attorney about the scope of the limitation.

H.   Attorney's fee provision

In most instances, a business can't recover its legal fees for a dispute unless the contract specifically allows for this recovery. The concept that each side should bear their own cost of litigation is called the American Rule. Some statutes and causes of action like fraud allow for the recovery of attorney's fees, but they are more likely to benefit your customer than you. Include an attorney's fee provision in your contract.

I. Severability clause

Sometimes a contract has a provision that the court can't or won't enforce. If the contract term isn't clear, a court can't enforce it. If a term is not allowable under the law, like a release of a future negligence claim in many states, then the court won't enforce it. Without a severability clause that provides the court will read the agreement as if the bad provision doesn't exist, the entire contract would be unenforceable. A severability provision allows the court to sever or cut the unenforceable provision from the document and save the remaining terms.

J. Joint drafting provision

In the event that a contract is unclear, the court reads the provision against the person who wrote the agreement. In a joint drafting provision, the parties acknowledge that the agreement was jointly drafted and the presumption against the writer of the agreement doesn't apply.

K. Any other provision required to comply with any law specific to your industry

The business's client contract needs special provisions if the business works with consumers or in another highly-regulated area of the law in order to meet the regulatory or statutory needs. For example, if the business manages health care data for a hospital or wellness clinic, its client contract needs provisions to comply with the Health Insurance Portability and Accountability Act. Many consumer protection laws allow the consumer a three-day "cool off" period to change his mind and cancel the contract without penalty. Check with an attorney about laws that are specific to your area of business to ensure that your contracts comply with them and any required provisions are included.

Don't Use Your Client's Contract

As tempting as it might be to use your client's agreement rather than pay for one of your own, especially when your business is just starting out, don't do so unless you must. The person who writes the contract controls the relationship. It's easier to modify proposed terms than to add new ones into a contract negotiation. Also, your client's contract was prepared by the client's attorney to protect the client, not your business. Draft the client service contract to give your business the maximum protection you can.

Promptly Respond to Customer Calls and Complaints

Most disputes can be headed off. A customer expects a quick response when he calls and a quicker response when he complains. In the end, a business is its customer relationships. Making your client feel as though he's your only customer goes a long way toward avoiding client-related landmines. Listen when a client complains. Sometimes all that's needed is an acknowledgment that the company delivered less than sterling service and a promise to do better. At other times, a business must take significant action to correct a problem. If the business has done something wrong, do everything you can to fix it.

Maintain Client Records

A business should maintain a record of all customer complaints and issues. The company should have a standard complaint form that employees complete when an issue arises.

The form's information section should include the customer's complete name and address, the location address if the business has more than one, the complaint details and the client's proposed resolution. The company should also secure all supporting documents from the client. Take photos of any claimed damage, if possible. Next, the form should have a company "proposed action" section, where the company outlines its response to the complaint, and a complaint resolution section indicating the response the client accepted.

At the end of the complaint process, the client should be asked to rate their experience with the company. If the company gets anything less than a ten out of ten for excellence, it needs to follow up with the client regarding what the company could do to make the experience a ten, or how it could respond better next time.

Creating a document that could be used against the company in later litigation might seem weird, but if the company follows its procedures for handling customer complaints litigation becomes less likely *and* the form may become the company's best defense. A parking garage customer complained that her car had been damaged while parked. Her parking ticket included an express waiver of liability. She was required to fill out the complaint and damage form and stated the car was not dented when she gave it to the attendant but was damaged when he returned it. More importantly, the parking attendant took pictures of the car and the claimed damage and noted that it wasn't a rainy day. The photos showed that the dent the client claimed the attendant put in her car was mud-splattered. When the case later went to trial, the court discounted the customer's testimony, found that the damage predated her parking the car and dismissed her claim.

Diamonds are a girl's best friend; documentation is a company's best friend. Even if a client never complains, having client records about what the company did may help if litigation ensues. If, despite the company's best efforts to craft a clear and enforceable agreement, the court finds the agreement unenforceable or the company can't prove the terms for a verbal agreement, the company may still recover the *value* of the services performed, assuming it can show that the client knew the company expected to be paid for its work (in legal mumbo jumbo, this is known as a *quantum meruit* claim). But the company will need records of the work and the market value.

"Value" is not necessarily what the company expected to receive on a contract basis, or its costs. As an example, an inexperienced landlord entered into a verbal lease with a tenant for an eighteen-month rental at twenty-five hundred dollars per month. Virginia law requires leases for more than a year to be in writing, so the handshake deal rental agreement resulted in no enforceable contract. The tenant stopped paying rent three months in, and the landlord sued for the unpaid rent and for possession of the property (legalese for the right to evict the tenant). The court found that the reasonable rental value of the property was fifteen hundred dollars and awarded damages based on this amount.

Don't Let Fear Make You Accept a Client You Shouldn't

We've all been there. Business is slowing down or we have an unexpected bill. Then the phone rings. It's a potential customer. The business is saved!

Or is it?

When you meet with the customer, you realize she's not your ideal client. Sometimes it's because the client can't afford you, or the services are a bit out of your business's sweet spot, or she doesn't listen to your advice, or the client just isn't a personality fit. For whatever reason, you know in the consultation that this isn't a client you should take on. But rather than trust your instincts and business sense, you let fear call the shots and you take the client.

Please stay strong.

Every time I've convinced myself to take a client I shouldn't, I've regretted it. Always. A prospective client, let's call him Scrooge, once asked me to reduce my hourly rate because his business had "lots of work" that needed to be done—the "make-it-up-in-volume" argument. I was willing to take the risk that the extra work wouldn't materialize and discounted my rate. Scrooge was high-maintenance, and we were on the phone for a half an hour a day, at least, until the first invoice went out. The problem was Scrooge never paid his bill on time, and, when I called to see where his payment was, he'd try to negotiate the invoice down even further. Dealing with Scrooge became such a hassle that I dreaded whenever I had to talk to him. Rather than continue the relationship, I fired him. Making that decision was nerve-racking; after all, some money was better than none, right?

Wrong.

That client didn't respect my time or expertise. The relationship wasn't going to improve over time, as the client would continue to expect the same or bigger discounts. By freeing up the time I was spending to work on this high-maintenance, low-pay client, I obtained two new clients who paid my regular rate and appreciated my efforts.

While some people advise firing ten percent of your customer base every year, I think having an arbitrary number is insane and possibly harmful for your business. But the sentiment is right. Regularly review your client relationships to ensure those relationships are good fits for your business. Not all work is good work. Don't let fear run your business. Trust that if you are serving the right customers, more of them will find you.

How to Avoid This Landmine

Managing the client relationship comes down to a few tips:

- Have a client contract.
  - Clearly set forth any contingencies or limitations on the scope of work.
  - Expressly waive warranties, if applicable.
  - Succinctly state your out clause.
- Don't use your client's contract if you don't have to.
- Respond to customer calls or complaints in a timely manner.
- Maintain client records.
- Don't let fear make your business decisions.

Understand that a client can get emotionally attached to their decisions or desired results and that it's your business's job to remove the emotion from the equation. This may mean that a client terminates the business relationship. Just remember that the worst thing you can hear a client say is, "I wish I'd listened to you."

CHAPTER 8

LANDMINE 7: Commingling, Or Embezzling, From Yourself

Your business's money isn't yours.

As strange as it may seem, the law considers your business a "person." A company owns property and other assets. It may use those assets as it sees fit to pursue its business objectives. A company must keep accurate financial and other records of its transactions. Certain accounting programs now have products aimed at entrepreneurs and businesses with single owners that encourage the use of corporate funds for personal debt and theoretically make it easier to document the difference between a true company expense and a personal one.

What most business owners don't think about is the fact that, because a company is a "person," an owner can steal from his business.

So, first, what is "commingling?"

When a business owner treats his business funds as his personal money, he is mixing the money or commingling. The most common ways to commingle are:

- Paying personal expenses with business funds or credit, and vice versa.

- Depositing business checks into your personal bank account.

- Transferring money between business and personal accounts.

A business owner is more at risk for accidently commingling when he operates his business out of his personal bank accounts.

Why is commingling a big deal?

Commingling funds can be unethical and sometimes illegal. Also, treating a business's assets as personal ones and personal debts as company ones can cause three distinct landmines: partner disputes, piercing the corporate veil and IRS issues.

Partner Disputes

One of the biggest disputes business owners have is about how to divide the money. Just because one partner is a sixty percent shareholder doesn't mean that the majority shareholder should run his personal expenses through the company. In one case I worked on, the majority shareholder, Shamus, had the company paying for his cell phone and car, which was probably okay, but the company also paid for Shamus's wife's, adult son's and adult daughter's cell phones, cars and rent, as well as lots of very expensive dinners. When pressed, Shamus would tell the other shareholders that the funds were debt repayment for loans he'd made to the company and the dinners were for "business development." Not only were there no documents showing the loans or funds transferred to the company, but also, the annual tax returns, which he had prepared, didn't show those payments as debt service; instead, those amounts were categorized as general business expenses. Shamus had given himself a one hundred percent raise with all his cash withdrawals and seriously jeopardized the company's health. The other owners refused to guarantee the next renewal of the business's line of credit, and the company folded.

In another case, the two owners, Brad and Jessica, were fifty-fifty partners—except Brad decided he was doing the lion's share of the work and deserved more. Without telling Jessica, Brad redirected company payments to his personal bank account. Jessica later learned from a vendor that payments were being made in cash to Brad for the company's goods. She checked the company's records. No cash deposits. Again, the confrontation over the use of the company's money destroyed the business.

Sometimes problems arise when company-to-owner transaction paperwork just isn't clear. A retired designer, Andy, bought an interest in a small staffing company. The company wasn't profitable, and over the years she loaned the company money and repaid the loans when there was sufficient cash to do so. While the other partner, Miranda, had access to the records, she never looked at them. After several years in business, Andy wanted to retire again, and Miranda wanted complete control over the company. They structured a deal, which would have been to everyone's benefit. The problem occurred when Miranda finally paid attention to the company's operations; she realized the company wouldn't survive without the no-interest financing Andy had provided, and that Miranda needed more money to keep the company operating. Miranda refused to honor her side of the stock transfer and alleged that Andy had committed fraud and stolen company funds. Andy now had a big problem, even though her loans had benefited the company for years, because she hadn't clearly documented the transactions and resolving the dispute required her to recreate those transactions.

While an owner is entitled to her percentage of the business's profit, problems can happen when one owner advances herself "profit" before any determination of profitability has been made. If she overdraws the later profit distribution, she might have violated her duties to her other partners and jeopardized the company's livelihood, and she will have to repay those amounts to the company for proper distribution.

Even when a company only has one owner, treating the company's money as the owner's money can cause significant problems.

Piercing the Corporate Veil

Incorporation generally protects the assets of the company's owners from the business's debts. This protection is called the "corporate shield" or "veil." Creditors usually ignore that man standing behind the curtain. However, there are things a business owner can do that allow the creditors to pull back (or pierce) the curtain (corporate veil): sign a guarantee of the company's debt; commit fraud; or commingle assets. I will not address the first two methods for piercing the corporate veil here. Think of the third basis—commingling assets—as "fraud light."

When a business owner commingles assets, that owner doesn't respect the difference between the company's separateness (assets and debts) and the owner's individuality (personal assets and debts). Small businesses are particularly at risk for making this mistake. When you start a business, the funds often come from your account and do so for a significant time. Also, the line between company and person is sometimes blurry. As an example, an entrepreneur uses her car to call on clients. Is the repair cost and gas for that vehicle really a company expense? Sadly, that answer is "it depends."

Let me step back. There is often nothing wrong with a business owner conducting business with his company or reimbursing business expenses. Even using a company credit card to pay a personal expense *might* not be a problem if handled properly (more on that in "How to Avoid This Landmine" at the end of this chapter). Problems arise when the transactions are numerous and the company classifies clearly personal ones as business expenses so that a court considers the company no more than the "alter ego" of its owner. In that case, the court can disregard the company's existence and its corporate shield to impose liability on the owner for a company debt.

It takes a lot of financial abuse or commingling before a court imposes such a harsh and extreme remedy, and not all states allow for piercing the corporate veil on the "alter ego" theory. I had a case where the one hundred percent owner of the company, Tully, promised my client, Hilary, a sales representative, a significant commission on her sales. They had many discussions, and Tully even presented Hilary with a commission agreement but refused to let her sign it because he wanted to "tweak" the document. Ultimately, he shorted Hilary over three hundred thousand dollars and used those funds to buy his new house.

When she sued to collect the commission due, she also asked the court to hold Tully liable for the debt because he'd used the company as his personal piggy bank. Discovery (the process of finding out about the other side's case and getting copies of their documents during a lawsuit) showed that the owner was paying for family vacations, household utilities, artwork for his house and charges at Neiman Marcus, Victoria's Secret, Abercrombie and Fitch and other high-end clothing stores with the company's credit card. The business tax returns declared these "business expenses." The court found that the company was nothing more than a front for Tully's personal dealings and pierced the corporate veil. Tully had made a very expensive decision to ignore the company's separate existence.

IRS Issues

Here's where things have the potential to get illegal. Fast. The Internal Revenue Service collects a fee on all income made by a company and its owners for the federal government. Trying to pass personal expenses off as business expenses is tax evasion and fraud. Misclassifying income as an expense improperly reduces the net revenues that the company and owners are taxed on.

For example, an entrepreneur, Ryan, forms a limited liability company (LLC) and has the company he works for pay his commissions to his LLC. Ryan transfers small amounts of money from the LLC to his personal bank account. However, the vast majority of his living expenses (utilities, personal credit cards, mortgage payment, meals and the like) are paid directly by the LLC. During the year, the LLC is paid over $200,000. Come the next April 15, the LLC files its income tax return showing $200,000 in gross income, $170,000 in "business expenses" and $30,000 in "profit." The LLC sends Ryan tax reporting documents for $30,000 of income. He then files his personal tax return and only declares $30,000 for income. He gets a tax refund from his estimated tax payments. The LLC is selected at random for a tax audit. During the audit, the LLC can't document its claimed expenses. Worse, the existing documentation shows most of its "expenses" were really payments on the entrepreneur's personal debt and income to him. Now there's an IRS problem.

At minimum, Ryan and his LLC are looking at a significant tax liability, interest and penalties. The IRS can also refer the matter for prosecution if it believes the misclassification of income as expenses was willful.

How to Avoid This Landmine

How does a business owner avoid the issues that come with commingling? The answer's surprisingly simple.

- Document all personal payments from company funds.

Paying personal obligations with company funds isn't a commingling problem *if* the transaction is reflected as an owner draw on the company's books and records and the owner recognizes that payment as income. Consider the difference between these two scenarios:

A.   Tax Free LLC pays eight thousand dollars for its owner Steve's vacation to Hawaii with his family. Tax Free declares the payment as an "expense" and deducts the eight thousand dollars from its tax returns.

B.   Tax Free pays eight thousand dollars for Steve's vacation to Hawaii with his family. Tax Free records the payment in its records as an "owner draw" or "owner distribution." Tax Free declares the eight thousand dollars as a profit payment to Steve on its tax returns. Steve declares the eight thousand dollars as income and pays the taxes on the amount.

In scenario A, Steve has embezzled from Tax Free and commingled assets. He leaves Tax Free and himself open to a later argument by a creditor that a court should pierce the corporate veil. They are also liable for the underpayment of taxes and risk penalties, fines, interest and criminal prosecution.

In Scenario B, Steve still gets his trip to Hawaii; he just has to pay taxes on the funds used for the trip. He's done nothing to weaken his corporate shield.

It may seem silly to write a company check to the owner, then have to wait for the check to clear before the owner can use "her" money. Taking the time to transfer funds creates a paper trail to document the movement of the money. Certain accounting software companies have new programs that make it easier for a solo businesses owner or entrepreneur to document the difference between business and personal expenses. Use them or other reasonable accounting methods to differentiate these transactions.

- Keep separate bank accounts.

It is much easier to inadvertently misclassify expenses if a business owner only has one bank account. When it comes time to categorize a particular expense, the owner or bookkeeper may not remember whether that specific transaction was personal or business. My best advice is to avoid this problem by having at least two checking accounts—one for business-only expenses and another for personal expenses.

- If you loan money to or borrow money from the business, sign a promissory note.

In the earlier example where Andy lent the company funds and repaid herself, she made a mistake by not drafting and signing promissory notes for the transactions. Again, when you're the only owner it may seem silly to undertake this step, but remember, if a creditor later tries to pierce the corporate veil, these promissory notes will help resist the creditor's efforts and give you an extra layer on the corporate shield.

As strange as it seems, some actions may be later viewed as stealing from your business. Financial shortcuts in moving money from the business's accounts to the owner's accounts can result in later difficulties. If your business partner has diverted too much of the company's revenue to his personal expenses, an owner dispute and corporate divorce is likely. Creditors may be able to circumvent the protection incorporation gave to your personal assets if the separateness of your business and personal assets and debts isn't maintained. Worse, the IRS might disallow the claimed business expenses and re-characterize those expenses as income to the business owner. When this happens, the business owner will face, at minimum, additional tax liability, penalties and interest. Don't take shortcuts with the business's finances. The price you might pay for doing so could be devastating.

CHAPTER 9

LANDMINE 8: Not Properly Using Restrictive Covenants

To Compete or Non-Compete; That is the Question.

ere's a business owner's nightmare: Claire owns a women's boutique and hired Karen to help her. The clients love Karen. Karen quits. Claire thinks nothing of it until she passes Karen's Emporium a block from her store and watches her clients going there instead of into her store. How do you protect your business from this heartache? Read on.

Employees are the group most likely to cause difficulties for your business. Why? Because they have access to varying levels of critical company information, and the laws surrounding the employer-employee relationship are many and complex. This chapter addresses issues that can arise when your employees have access to your company's trade secrets and confidential information and discusses what steps a company can take to protect itself.

Confidential information, or information the company wishes to keep secret or restricted, isn't always a trade secret. A trade secret is any valuable commercial information that provides a business an edge or advantage over its competitors who don't have that information and when attempts have been made to keep the information secret. State law provides some protection. Most states follow the Uniform Trade Secrets Act, which states that it protects information, including but not limited to, a formula, pattern, compilation, program, device, method, technique, or process, that:

> "1. Derives independent economic value, actual or potential, from not being generally known to, and not being readily ascertainable by proper means by, other persons who can obtain economic value from its disclosure or use, and

> 2. Is the subject of efforts that are reasonable under the circumstances to maintain its secrecy."

A non-exhaustive list of trade secrets under the uniform act includes inventions, ideas, compilations of data, any useful formula, plan, pattern, process, program, tool, technique, mechanism, compound or device that is not generally known or readily ascertainable by the public. Customer lists, negotiated vendor discounts and a company's financial information are likely trade secrets. While complete secrecy isn't required, the business has to take reasonable steps to protect its trade secrets from misuse or improper disclosure. What is reasonable will vary on a case-by-case basis, but having a written confidentiality policy or agreement in place is important, if not required.

This legal framework leads to one of my favorite client or potential client questions: Do you have a form non-competition agreement? And, can the client have it yesterday?

A restrictive covenant is any agreement or provision that prevents one party to the agreement from taking some action. The three most common restrictive covenants in the employer-employee relationship are confidentiality, competition and solicitation limitations. A word of caution about this chapter: State law controls whether there can be post-employment restrictions on an ex-employee's activities and what those restrictions might include. Some states prohibit these restrictions altogether, while others allow restrictions when a co-owner leaves the business. Still other states allow reasonable post-employment restrictions. This section is only a general overview. Check your state's laws to determine what rules apply to post-employment restrictions.

Confidentiality Agreements

State laws protect a company from the use and misappropriation of its trade secrets even without a written agreement between the company and its employees. However, a company often wants to protect confidential material that may have no independent economic value or otherwise doesn't fit the trade secret definition under the uniform act. What happens when the information is just sensitive, but doesn't meet the definition of a trade secret? The company might be left with its assets exposed. How do you avoid this risk?

To protect confidential information, you need a written agreement.

The employee signs an agreement and a handbook with a confidentiality provision. Here's a word of caution about solely relying on a provision in a handbook: While the handbook provision shows the company took action to protect its information, a court may later determine that the handbook provision isn't as enforceable against the employee as a contract. A definition of confidential information is defined by agreement and can include:

> economic, commercial marketing, client information, financial information that is confidential or proprietary in nature, and all Trade Secrets as that term is defined under state law.

Most courts agreed that confidential information doesn't include information which is or becomes generally available to the public other than as a result of a disclosure by the employee or any of its representatives; or is required to be disclosed by the employee due to governmental regulatory, court order or judicial process.

Trade secret and confidentiality cases often focus on whether the information is subject to reasonable efforts to maintain its secrecy. Disclosures of the information must be made in implied or expressed confidence. This means you either need an agreement to keep the information private or you need to tell someone the information in circumstances that make it clear the information should remain private. Obviously, there's lots of room to fight about whether there was an implied confidence so having a contract expressly stating this protection is preferred.

Take these four steps to protect your business's information from misuse:

- Restrict access to the information in both written and electronic form to "need to know" individuals. Use a computer system or programs with different levels of access for different categories of employees.

- Have a confidentiality policy in your employee hand-book.

- Have employment agreements with nondisclosure and confidentiality provisions tailored to each position's access to the confidential information.

- Have nondisclosure agreements with business partners, licensees, franchisees or anyone with access who has no independent duty of nondisclosure.

Non-competition Provisions

A non-competition provision is what most people mean when they ask about a restrictive covenant. A true non-competition provision prevents an employee from working in the same business in a specific geographic area for a period of time after his employment ends. The rationale behind these agreements is that a company wants to secure the parts of its operations and client relationships the former employee worked on without interference from that individual.

Okay, I get that.

However, there's a fairly large "but" that argues against the company's interests: the employee's right to earn a living. Because these agreements limit a former employee's rights, they are restrictions on trade and are disfavored by the courts. Your state's law determines what specific restrictions are permissible.

Employees owe their employer a duty of loyalty and can't profit at their employer's expense. If an employee comes across work his employer can do, then he must turn that work over to his employer. For example, Heidi sells gutters for Shiny Gutters Inc. Every once and a while, rather than give the potential customer a quote from Shiny Gutters, Heidi writes a customer a quote for her side business and diverts the work. Heidi has breached her duty of loyalty to the company. Shiny Gutters can sue Heidi for breach of her duty of loyalty, and possibly other claims *even if the company doesn't have a non-competition agreement with Heidi.*

This changes, however, when Heidi leaves the company. When Heidi employment ends, so does her duty of loyalty. She's free to compete with her former employer unless the competition is based on her misconduct while employed, or prohibited by a specific statute, *or* Heidi signed a valid non-competition agreement.

What makes a non-competition agreement valid?

Glad you asked.

Different states use different words to phrase the test for a valid non-competition agreement, but generally, all courts look at similar issues. Courts consider the restriction's geographic scope, time period and functional scope when determining if the restriction is valid. Litigation often focuses on the functional scope, which is further broken down to whether or not the restriction is narrowly tailored to meet a company's legitimate business interests. The second test focuses on what the company does, what the employee did for the company, what information the employee could access and how the restriction affects the employee's ability to make a living once he is no longer employed.

Courts vary on how rigidly they construe these elements and whether they have the power to modify the restriction. Virginia leans strongly against enforcement. Recently, the Virginia Supreme Court ruled that if the restriction *might* prevent the former employee from taking a non-competing job at a competitor then the restriction is unenforceable as not being "narrowly tailored." Similarly, if your company uses the same post-employment restrictions for its receptionist as it does for its COO, it's likely that a Virginia court won't enforce this one-size-fits-all restriction. Worse, Virginia law doesn't allow a court to modify a restriction to make it enforceable. Maryland is more forgiving, and can, in the proper cases, modify the provision to make it enforceable. But remember, if you overreach, your business could end up unprotected.

Let's use an example to make this issue more concrete. Under these facts, the provision below is *unlikely* to be enforceable: An employee/shareholder, Carla, worked for a company that sold one brand of cigar, and her territory only covered the East Coast of the United States. The general acquisition cycle of a customer was a year, and customers signed a twelve-month distribution agreement. Carla's agreement had the following restrictive covenant:

> For a period of three (3) years after the termination or expiration of this Agreement Employee shall not, directly or indirectly own, manage, control, be employed by, participate in, or be connected in any manner with ownership, management, operation or control of any business similar to the type of business conducted by Employer at the time this Agreement terminates. [15]

---

[15] *Simmons v. Miller*, 261 Va. 561, 580 (2001).

Why is this provision unenforceable?

The restriction goes too far in every area.

Geographic Scope: While the employee can rely on the skills and experience she acquired at her former firm when selling tobacco products in Texas, she's not leveraging the contacts she made while working for the company. Since the employee only worked on the East Coast, a restriction that covers the entire United States is broader than necessary for the employer to protect its legitimate business interest.

Scope of Activities Restricted or Functional Restrictions: The functional scope of the restriction is too broad for two reasons. First, the employee only sold one brand of cigar but would be prevented from selling *any tobacco product* such as cigarettes, e-cigarettes or snuff. The employer has no legitimate reason to prevent the employee from working in these non-competing tobacco related fields. Second, the restriction prevents her from working in a non-competitive position and from owning stock in a publicly traded company with some connection with the tobacco industry. Owning stock in Philip Morris violates this provision. The employer has no legitimate interest in preventing the employee from investing in a publicly traded company. The employer has no legitimate interest in preventing the former employee from being a janitor at a company that sells competing cigars or from selling e-cigarettes. Because the range of prohibited activities is far wider than the company's actual business, this restriction is unlikely to be enforced.

Time Limitations: The length of the restriction must be reasonably related to the company's business. In the above example, it takes the company up to two years to develop a lead, and a customer contract is for one year. A three-year restriction which allows the employee's successor to close any leads and have one renewal of those client contracts is more likely to be upheld than the five-year restriction the company has included.

This restriction prevents the employee from working anywhere in her chosen field. Because the restriction is much broader than needed to protect a legitimate business interest of the company and is very harsh on the employee's ability to earn a living, a court is unlikely to enforce the restriction.

But given the right facts, this provision might be enforced. If the employee was the Chief Executive Officer in charge of all United States operations for a company that sells a wide variety of tobacco products and the average client contract is four years in length, the provision would be reasonably related to the company's legitimate business interests and could be enforced.

Now compare the bad provision, above, to the one below:

In this case, the employee/shareholder, Robert, is a partner in an executive medical practice in Anytown, USA. The practice advertises for clients within a seventy-five-mile radius and most of the clients come from within a fifty-mile radius. The client acquisition cycle is six to twelve months, and clients sign a twelve-month service agreement. Robert's restrictive agreement states:

> During the term of this Agreement and for a period of two (2) years after the termination of this Agreement for whatever reason, Doctor will not, without the prior consent of Employer, directly or indirectly engage in the practice of medicine and/or surgery that competes with the Practice in a

competitive position within 75 miles of the city of ANYTOWN, USA.

The Doctor will not violate this provision solely by owning a non-controlling interest in a publicly traded company or a passive interest of less than 5 percent of a non-publicly traded company.

If Doctor engages in the practice of medicine in violation of this covenant, then Doctor must pay the Employer, as liquidated damages, five annual payments in an amount equal to 20 percent of the total taxable compensation received by Doctor from Employer for the twelve-month period immediately preceding the termination of Doctor's employment. Such annual payments will commence upon termination of this agreement and continue on each anniversary thereof until five annual payments have been made.

Why is this provision more likely to be enforceable?

Geographic Scope: The seventy-five-mile radius is tied to where the company advertises and draws clients. This portion of the restriction is likely to be deemed reasonable.

Scope of Activities Restricted or Functional Restrictions: The functional scope of the restriction is also likely to be enforceable. First, the employee is only prohibited from working for a "competitive company" in a "competitive position." The employee could work for a competitive business as its director of marketing rather than as a doctor and surgeon. Remember, the agreement must define what "competitive business" and "competitive position" mean or face litigation over those terms.

The restriction also carves out passive investments. Even though moving his practice seventy-six miles from where he used to work might seem harsh, it's a reasonable restriction to protect the business he's leaving.

Time Limitations: It takes the company up to a year to develop a lead and a customer contract is for one year. A two-year restriction allows the employee's successor to close any leads and have one renewal of those client contracts, and is likely to be upheld.

Because this restriction is narrowly tailored and imposes a reasonable restriction on the employee's ability to earn a living, a court is likely to enforce the restriction. Another interesting thing this provision does is establish an agreed amount of damages (the amount of the doctor's compensation from the employer during his last year of work paid over five years). Assuming the court upholds the restriction, the liquidated damages provision means the company doesn't have to prove its actual damages (how much money it lost) from the violation, just that the damages assessed are a reasonable estimate of the damage it might have sustained.

Non-solicitation Provisions

Often a company only needs an agreement that prevents the employee from working for a company client or someone who was a prospect when the employee's employment ended. A non-solicitation provision is a sub-species of a non-competition provision. Non-solicitation provisions prevent a former employee from poaching clients or other employees and are judged by the same standard as non-competition agreements. These provisions are more likely to be enforced because the functional scope is so very narrow. Again, overreaching will invalidate the provision. An example of overreaching is when the employee only had access to or knowledge of a limited segment of the company's clients, but the restriction prohibits providing competing services to all clients. Similarly, a restriction that prevents an IT support employee from selling branded cookies to a company customer is probably overreaching.

A form non-competition provision is unlikely to be worth the paper it's written on. By definition, a "form" is too generic to satisfy the court. If you think your business needs protection from its former employees, you should meet with an attorney to determine what protection is best. The attorney must understand your business to recommend whether or not you need a non-competition agreement and its scope. Non-competition agreements can be a great tool to protect your business, but remember, you want a custom fit and not an off-the-rack agreement.

Because much of the law covering restrictive covenants is created by the court, their rules are subject to change. You should review your restrictive covenants at least every two to three years to ensure that they are still enforceable. Otherwise you might end up like one Virginia company that relied on a case that enforced a particular non-competition provision in 1989, only to have the same provision determined unenforceable due to changes in the law when it was next contested in 2011 [16]. Employment law is not fix-it-and-forget-it. It's a living, breathing dragon that will burn your business to the ground if you don't check on it every few years.

---

[16] Compare, Home Paramount Pest Control Cos. v. Shaffer, 282 Va. 412, 718 S.E.2d 762 (2011) with Paramount Termite Control Co. v. Rector, 238 Va. 171 (1989),

In conclusion, employees pose a unique risk to your business because they have access to its information and clients. State law provides some protection for trade secrets. Generally speaking, these protections won't go far enough to protect all the information a business deems confidential. In that case, have a written confidentiality agreement with key employees. If your state allows it, key employees should also have post-employment restrictions on their ability to offer similar services to the company's clients or, in appropriate cases, to compete in the company's region. These steps will help you protect your investment and retain your clients once your employees leave your company.

How to Avoid This Landmine

- Even if your state has a Trade Secrets Act, have a separate confidentiality agreement with your employees that broadens the protected information to meet your business needs.

- If your state allows post-employment restrictions on trade (non-competition agreements), make sure that the restrictions are reasonably related to both:
  - The information the employee learned about or had access to in the business and
  - The company's legitimate business interests. If you overreach, you'll have no protection at all.

- Update and enforce these policies.

CHAPTER 10

LANDMINE 9: Things Your Employees or Contractors Do That Will Get You Sued

Sometimes the law is less about what it says than about what people think it says.

Running your business ethically isn't as clear-cut as it should be. Conflicting laws and constantly changing workplace environments make legal mistakes harder to avoid, detect and resolve. Today, ignorance creates liability. Untrained managers and employees with good intentions can cause more risk than obvious bad actors. Learn how to identify and prevent the unintentional yet dangerous actions employees take every day that erode the protections and standards you and your human resources department put in place for the company and its employees.

The state and federal laws that address interactions between employees and employers read like a dinner menu written in a language created for a science fiction show: ADA, EPA, ERA,

ERISA, FCRA, FLSA, FMLA, HIPAA, IRCA, LLFPA, OSHA, OWPA, SOX and USERRA, just to name a few.

Whether or not many of these laws apply to your company will depend on its size, while coverage by others will depend on what services your company offers or on its revenue. Often more than one law will apply to the same situation. Laws may also govern how you interact with your customers. It's probably not surprising, then, that in this arena you can trip over a legal landmine long before you know it's there.

Even if an employee can't sign a contract for the company, the employee can still cost you. Lots. Some of what an employee can do to create liability should be obvious. Other actions … not so much.

So, how can your employees get you sued?

A word of warning: No single chapter can cover all of the possible rules you have to follow and pitfalls that come with employees. My goal is to alert you to the most common mistakes you might not know you or your employees are making.

Companies Can Be Sued for What Their Employees Tell a Customer or What the Customer Assumes

Your employees are the first line of contact between your customers and your company, so it may not surprise you that you can be sued for anything your employees say or do in your name. But sometimes you can be responsible for things your client only assumed.

Companies that work with consumers are subject to various state and federal consumer protection laws. Essentially, these laws prohibit using false or misleading statements in a company's dealings with a consumer (an individual rather than a company) for a consumer purchase (related to family or household needs rather than business needs). Even if your company's business is company-to-company, it can run into trouble if the other business perceives that your company has misrepresented its products or services. Companies can only act through their employees, so anything your employees do might open the business to litigation and liability risks.

Your employees are the public face of your company. Your sales staff, whether called that or not, finds new customer pipelines, mines those pipelines and communicates with your customers. What your salesperson says matters. And can get you sued.

When an employee lies to a customer, the company is unlikely to escape liability.

For most of us, "fraud" happens when someone lies to us. Courts look deeper into the statement before determining if fraud occurred. In the law, "fraud" is when a person makes a misstatement of a material fact, whether knowingly or with a reckless disregard for whether or not the statement is true, intending for someone else to rely on the misrepresentation, and that person actually does rely on the misstatement. Sometimes the line between a lie and an opinion is razor thin.

When a salesperson says that her company's new widget is the best thing since sliced bread, she's engaged in "puffery" and not making a material misstatement. Also, we rarely believe salespeople when they extol the virtues of their products. We know salespeople engage in hyperbole, saying things such as, "Our product is a million times better than ..."

Winning a fraud claim is difficult. Fraud must be proved by "clear and convincing evidence." What's that mean? Well, it's not about a mathematically precise percentage. Most civil cases (people suing over money) are determined by a "preponderance of the evidence," which means the jury or judge is something over fifty percent sure that the plaintiff was harmed and it was the defendant's fault. A tie usually, but not always, goes to the plaintiff. In a criminal case, a jury must acquit the defendant unless they are sure "beyond a reasonable doubt" that the defendant committed the crime he's charged with. "Beyond a reasonable doubt" is something like 99.99 percent sure. "Clear and convincing evidence" in a civil case is more than a "preponderance of the evidence" but less than "beyond a reasonable doubt." The jury must firmly believe the defendant lied about a fact and that the plaintiff believed the lie and acted in a certain way because she believed the lie. Whether the percentage of surety is seventy-five, eighty or ninety-five percent remains unclear. As I said, math has little to do with these standards. Let's just agree that it's hard to prove fraud.

But you can still get sued because of what your employee tells a customer, even when your employee tells the truth.

In one case, a homeowner, Ernesto, sued a landscape supply business, Ground Cover Experts Co., alleging that the product sold, labeled as "organic topsoil," wasn't actually "organic" or "topsoil." Not only did Earnesto want back the five hundred dollars he paid for the soil, but he also wanted Ground Cover to pay to aerate and seed his lawn, for the new topsoil he had trucked in, and for legal fees (for the lawyer he didn't hire) and punitive damages (additional money awarded not to make the plaintiff whole but to punish the defendant). Ernesto claimed the company's salesperson said the soil was "organic" and would come from the local area. The issue was: What did the phrase "organic topsoil" mean? Yup, we were fighting over dirt. (There are days I love my job.)

Ernesto sued Ground Cover for twenty-five thousand dollars, as much as he could in that court. His argument was that "organic topsoil" was dark brown to black in color, and what was delivered had a red hue. (Virginia's native soil has a lot of clay and a resulting red tint. Most yards in the Northern Virginia area are fifty to sixty percent clay.). Because Ernesto's expectation of what he could win was unrealistic, settlement was impossible. Also, it would cost Ground Cover less to pay a lawyer to fight the case then to pay the unhappy customer.

Ernesto brought baggies of dried-out brown dirt, which he testified was a sample of the "organic topsoil" delivered two years earlier, and a black substance he claimed was "organic topsoil" to the trial. Ground Cover hired a dirt expert (yes, they exist) who testified that the dark black stuff found in many commercial products labeled "organic topsoil" was actually peat humus from Pennsylvania mushroom farms. Who knew, right? (This is one reason I love being a lawyer. I love learning facts that I'd never come across if it weren't for my clients. I can now also tell you how much sand an ideal soil sample should have in it.) The expert owned the company that had processed the soil and testified that his company had mixed the raw soil with compost. Ernesto meant one thing by "organic topsoil," i.e., the black peat humus, and Ground Cover meant something else, i.e., reddish Virginia soil mixed with compost.

Ultimately, the judge ruled that soil, almost by definition, was "organic," Ground Cover had delivered what its employee promised and Ernesto was not entitled to a judgment. Because an employee tried to describe organic soil, a five hundred-dollar sale cost Ground Cover almost ten times that amount in litigation expenses.

Your employees must have a script to use when talking to customers or a FAQ section on your website to which they can refer customers. Scripting the answers to common questions will help protect you against later claims and enhance quality control. The company might have avoided its lawsuit if every employee had said that organic topsoil was a mix of local soil and compost with, usually, a brown or red tint. Having a standard policy and definition gives you another layer of protection. A successful plaintiff must prove that your employee violated your policy, which violation might mean the employee was "outside the scope of his responsibility" and the company isn't responsible for the employee's bad act.

Employees must know which questions they can answer and which questions to pass on to someone in a superior position. As a best practices matter, you want employees to take notes on every prospective client and client interaction they have. While the documentation process used to be burdensome, modern technology gives us no excuse for laziness. But failing to document these interactions is not only laziness, it leaves the company open to possible litigation.

Companies can be liable not just for what their employees say, but also what they write in emails. More cases turn on the email and text message correspondence between the parties before the litigation arises. What was said during the transaction is more telling than anything the parties will say in court. Verbal agreements are now often easier to prove based on email communications regarding the deal. But this also means that litigation risks are higher.

A company's manager received a racially insensitive email from a third party, then shared the email with another company executive. One of the employees, of Afghan origin, was put on notice that he would be fired due to unsatisfactory job performance if he didn't improve. He alleged that the company's warning and ultimate termination of his employment was due to his ethnicity, a trait protected under federal and state anti-discrimination laws. Even though the subject of the "joke" email was of African American origin, the former employee tried to use the email to show management was bigoted. The email was the only evidence to support the former employee's testimony of bias and a hostile work environment. One stray insensitive email is unlikely to prove discrimination, but in this case it was enough to cost the company tens of thousands of dollars defending the litigation.

How do you avoid these landmines?

- Have a script for sales employees to use with customers, potential and actual.

- Have a written policy covering the appropriate use of electronic communications.

- Have and enforce a retention policy for electronic communications. Nothing is worse than not having a critical email that the other side has and you don't. Trust me on this.

Companies Can Be Sued for an Employee's Social Media Posts

The old marketing models are dead. It used to be that you could run ads in the Yellow Pages (yes, I know, I'm dating myself) and magazines and on television and have a strong marketing platform.

Not anymore.

Computers revolutionized the world and how we do business. We interact more on social media every day. We try to cram meaning into and make connection with 140-character tidbits. Failing to have a social media presence literally means failure in business. People don't turn to the Yellow Pages as their primary source of finding a company to do business with. We look up what we want on our mobile devices and computers. Companies scramble for content for their websites, social media pages and blogs—content that can lead you directly into three legal landmines: defamation, client disengagement and copyright infringement.

But how?

A. Defamation

A review or online post can be slanderous. You can be legally responsible for damages even if the subject of the statement can't show any actual damages.

Okay. Let's back up a second.

Originally, three types of claims arose from false statements made to third parties (not the speaker or the person the statement is about): slander, defamation and libel. The legal standards for proving these claims were slightly different. Many states have merged these three similar claims into one. Defamation, also known as slander or libel, is the act of making and publishing an untrue statement of fact about a person that damages the other person's reputation. In states which still recognize a distinction between slander and libel, slander is an oral statement; libel is a printed statement. Sometimes the untrue statement has the potential to cause so much harm (such as when it accuses someone of committing a crime, having a sexually transmitted or other feared and contagious disease or being unable to perform their occupation) that the court can award damages (money to make the injured party whole) even if that person can't prove any actual loss from the statements.

An untrue statement of fact about someone or some company posted on a social media site can support a defamation claim.

As an example, suppose your employee posts a false review of your competitor. Online forums like Yelp! now have to disclose who the anonymous poster is when ordered by the court. Your employee's anonymous post won't stay that way for long. You'll be defending a lawsuit for at least defamation and, possibly, intentional interference with business relationships based on the false review. An interference claim arises when an individual, knowing of a business relationship likely to continue between two other individuals, uses improper means to disrupt that relationship. Fraud—the false post—and defamation are improper means. When the competitor proves your employee's post costs them a large contract, your company could pay very large damages, even if your company didn't get the contract.

B.   Client Disengagement

Let me tell you a dirty secret.

Your company will be judged by what your *employees* post on their *personal* social media sites. Because clients often want to connect outside the previously normal workweek paradigm, clients can "friend" and "follow" (but not stalk) your company and its employees on social media platforms. Your company may be seen as holding or at least supporting the views stated by its employees on their individual sites.

One company, Conference Pro, holds an annual conference where attendee networking and connections are highly encouraged and are a strong selling point of the conference. To foster the connections, Conference Pro hosts an event-specific Facebook page for attendees. A registered attendee, Gwen, connected with a company employee, Brandon. Brandon posted a quasi-political comment on his personal page. Some *comments* on his post were radical and offensive. Gwen contacted Conference Pro because she no longer felt safe coming to the conference based on what a non-attendee/non-employee posted on Brandon's social media feed. As a matter of customer service and public relations, Conference Pro refunded Gwen's registration. Because Brandon didn't monitor and take down the offensive post on his *personal page*, Conference Pro immediately lost over a thousand dollars. Worse, most customers attend an average of three conferences, purchase several hundred dollars' worth of additional materials at the conference and refer other attendees. The company's actual loss was likely over ten thousand dollars because of a comment on an employee's personal post on his personal social media page.

C.   Copyright Infringement

The Internet has confused people about copyright laws. People assume that because a photo or item is posted they can copy and paste that item somewhere else. Problem is, it's likely they can't.

Copyright infringement happens when someone uses content that is copyrighted by others without their permission and interferes with the exclusive rights granted to the copyright holder, usually the creator of the work, including the right to sell, reproduce, distribute, display or perform the protected work or to make derivative works. There are limits on copyright. Contrary to common wisdom, ideas aren't copyrightable. If I have an idea for a purple unicorn story and tell a good friend, she's free to use the idea and write her own story. Copyright law protects the *expression* of that idea, in other words, the story itself. In the United States, the two purple unicorn stories must be substantially similar for a copyright violation to occur. So, if my purple unicorn is a devil beast and my friend's is the more typical savior type of beastie, it's unlikely her work will infringe on my copyright.

Another concept in copyright law is "fair use." Under certain circumstances, copyrighted material can be used without infringing on the owner's rights. This is a limited right to comment on, criticize or parody a copyrighted work (called a "transformational use"). Stanford University has a wonderful article on "fair use" and Columbia University has a Fair Use Checklist. The United States Copyright Office also maintains a database of court cases considering fair use exception. You can find links to all of these resources at my website, www.AttorneyNancyGreene.com/resources.

Factors considered in whether the use is fair include the purpose and nature of the use (is it transformational; is it commercial or noncommercial), the nature of the copyrighted work (is it factual or creative), how much of the work is used and the effect of the use on the market for the original work. "Good faith," a nebulous factor defined by the courts, is also considered. Many sitcoms avoid infringing on copyrights because they are parodying the original material or person. Use connected with scholarship and research is often not a violation of copyright laws when the use is designed to educate and inform. Infringement cases are all factually specific, and the decisions are based on the particular situations presented to the court.

Violation cases usually start with a "cease and desist" letter demanding that the infringing party stop using the copyrighted material. *If your business ever receives one of these letters, consult an attorney immediately.*

Not all cease and desist letters have merit. Sometimes the party sending the letter is just using its perceived clout to bully. In 2013, a cease and desist letter and its response went viral. The Town of West Orange, New Jersey sent a cease and desist letter to a resident, Jake, who had started a website with rudimentary information about the town. He received a letter from the Township's counsel arguing that the website infringed on the town's name and "may be a violation of the Township's federally protected rights." The town demanded the site be taken down and the domain name turned over to the town. Rather than get scared, he got an attorney. Stephen B. Kaplitt, Esquire's response to the cease and desist letter was hilarious. To see the response and more on the case, please visit my website, www.AttorneyNancyGreene.com/resources.

Let's assume though, that the cease and desist letter has merit. If the parties aren't able to resolve the dispute, litigation is likely. Penalties for copyright infringement can be stiff and include the actual damages sustained by the copyright holder, statutory damages of $200 to $150,000 for each work infringed, attorney's fees and costs, a court order to stop the infringing activity, impounding of the infringing work and yes, even jail.

When your employees post to social media or create marketing materials on your behalf, you need to ensure that you aren't inadvertently violating someone's copyright. This is a highly specialized area of the law. To avoid this landmine, ensure that your employees are purchasing the proper licenses for anything used or posted on the company's behalf. If you are unsure if you've complied with copyright law, consult with an attorney.

How do you avoid these landmines?

- Have a written policy covering appropriate use of third-party materials in the company's communications and social media.

- Monitor your employee's social media posts for the company and their personal posts.

- Verify that the proper licenses to and permissions to use potentially copyrighted materials have been obtained before any third-party material or photo is used.

Companies Can Be Sued When Their Employees Are Too Forthcoming ... with Their Former Employer's Trade Secrets or Other Confidential Information

New employees want to make a good impression. They want to contribute to the company's well-being. We hire them because we expect them to add value. Sometimes, though, an employee can be too helpful.

A trade secret is any information with commercial value (worth money) because the information isn't generally known to the public or your competitors. This can include customer lists, pricing lists, vendor discounts and business strategies. Most states have laws that specify what constitutes a trade secret. On the other hand, confidential information is much broader in scope and often is a matter of contract. Always ask a new hire if she signed a confidentiality agreement. Even when the new hire says no, remember that the employee may not remember signing a specific document in the stack she received when her last company hired her.

As tempting as it may be to take advantage of the situation when your new hire comes to you with your competitor's strategic business plan for the next three years, you need to tell the employee to destroy the document and not use it. If you use the other company's information you will be sued—even if you didn't know the information came from them.

How do you avoid this landmine?

Ask.

One of your interview questions should be, "Are you bound by any confidentiality agreement with any employer you worked for in the last five years?" Why five years? Because that time period is likely the outer edge of a non-competition/non-solicitation agreement. Also, trade secrets are only protected while they have commercial value. Most information is "stale"—meaning it has no monetary or commercial value—after five years. Most. The time frame isn't a guarantee, but if litigation occurs, the fact you investigated a possible claim might help your defense. Also, remember that employees rarely remember what they've signed during their employment, especially if the document was given to them with their new-hire paperwork. Take any "no" to this question with a bucket of salt.

NAVIGATING LEGAL LANDMINES

Ask where the information or documents came from if your new employee comes to you with a bunch of data or forms. It's not all right to accept and use the documents unless you can confirm that the information isn't a protected trade secret. Using someone else's customer list or pricing structure is an invitation to litigation. Just *don't* do it.

Employees Who Discriminate or Create a Hostile Work Environment Will Get You Sued

Once you have an employee, your company is covered by anti-discrimination laws. State law generally covers you from your first employee to your fourteenth. Federal law will apply from your fifteenth employee on. The federal law designed to prevent discrimination and harassment is Title VII of the Civil Rights Act of 1968 (Title VII). Special provisions apply for the government and for schools, but most companies are covered by Title VII. Most state anti-discrimination laws are patterned after Title VII, but sometimes the coverage or the damages your employees can recover differ. Under the District of Columbia Human Rights Act (D.C.'s version of Title VII), sexual orientation is protected, while it isn't under Title VII or under Virginia or Maryland law. In Virginia, the damages a plaintiff can recover under the Virginia Human Rights Act are very limited. Also, other laws prevent discrimination based on other characteristics such as disabilities (the Americans with Disabilities Act, or ADA) or genetics (the Genetic Information Nondiscrimination Act, or GINA). Because Title VII has a broader effect, I'll focus solely on it in this section.

A company must try to prevent and stop illegal harassment and discrimination. If you don't monitor your workplace and take steps to appropriately address complaints of harassment or discrimination, you are looking at a complaint to the EEOC followed by litigation.

I will only give you a few quick tips on how to manage your workplace to minimize harassment or discrimination claims since I've covered this issue in another landmine module.

A.   Understand the Protected Classifications Under the Law

Not all traits or beliefs are protected. Socioeconomic status isn't protected. Youth isn't protected but "old" age is. The following is a list of some of the protected classifications and the related federal laws:

Characteristic	Definition	Law
Ethnicity	Ancestry, culture or linguistic characteristics common to a specific ethnic group	Title VII
Race or Color	Blacks, whites, persons of Latino or Asian origin or descent and indigenous Americans (Eskimos, Native Hawaiians, Native Americans)	Title VII
National Origin	Birthplace or birthplace of ancestors	Title VII
Sex	Gender or pregnancy related	Title VII Equal Pay Act
Religion	All aspects of religious observance, practice and belief	Title VII
Age	Individuals 40 and older	Age Discrimination Act of 1967
Disability	Physical or mental impairments that limit one or more major life functions, history of this type of impairment or perception of this type of impairment	ADA; Rehabilitation Act (Federal Employees only) Family Medical Leave Act (FLSA)
Genetics	DNA and other genetic information including predispositions to certain illnesses or conditions	GINA

Until the early 2000's, courts didn't recognize discrimination claims made by a member of the "majority" classification. A white male was unlikely to prevail on a claim for discrimination when he was passed over for promotion in favor of an African American woman. However, the modern trend is to recognize so-called reverse discrimination where the majority class can state a claim that the employer prefers the minority classification based on that trait.

B.   Understand What Is Prohibited and What Isn't

Discrimination occurs when an employer prefers or penalizes one group of people over another based on a protected trait. Common wisdom may indicate that every racially insensitive comment or sexual innuendo is unlawful. Title VII *does not* guarantee a politically correct workplace where nary a profanity will be uttered.

What is protected, then?

Essentially, employment decisions such as hiring, firing, promoting, recruitment, testing, or fringe benefits or any other terms and conditions of employment can't be based on a protected classification. Employers also can't retaliate or take adverse job actions against individuals who complain of discrimination, participate in a discrimination investigation or oppose a discriminatory practice.

The one very limited exception to these rules is when the trait or lack thereof is a job requirement. Certain federal contracts can only be performed by American citizens because of national security concerns. In that limited case, an employer could refuse to hire a non-American citizen for the position without violating the anti-discrimination laws. Similarly, if the employee will load a truck, and regularly lifting one hundred pounds is a valid job requirement, then without violating the ADA the employer can refuse to hire someone for the position who can only lift five to ten pounds infrequently.

There are two types of discrimination and sexual harassment: *quid pro quo* and hostile work environment. A typical *quid pro quo* (literally, "something for something") sexual harassment occurs when a workplace benefit is conditioned or denied based on the granting of a sexual favor. While I'd love to say this form of discrimination no longer exists, I can't. However, cases of overt sexual harassment or discrimination are not as common as they once were.

The other kind of discrimination, hostile work environment, occurs when the discrimination is sufficiently pervasive and overt that it changes the nature of the workplace. Courts acknowledge that not all workplaces meet some ideal standard. Stray comments aren't enough to support a hostile work environment claim. A stand-alone occurrence of a coworker or even a management team member asking another worker out for drinks isn't a harassment violation. When that flirtation becomes both constant and unwelcome, a hostile work environment is likely to occur. The court will view the conduct on a subjective (how the employee perceived the conduct) and objective (how the average reasonable person would view the conduct) standard. The line between actionable conduct and non-actionable conduct isn't always clear.

C. Have A Written Anti-Harassment or Anti-Discrimination Policy

The anti-discrimination laws are remedial in nature, meaning they are designed to prevent and correct unlawful conduct.

Having a written anti-harassment and anti-discrimination policy is the first step in preventing and defending against these claims. Have a reporting policy by which the employee has a duty to report discrimination that happens to her or that she witnesses, and have a meaningful way for the employee to report the misconduct. Employees must take advantage of a company's legitimate reporting channels to maintain a later claim unless doing so would be objectively futile. These policies are your first line of defense against discrimination in the workplace.

D.   Enforce Your Policy

A policy does your company no good if you ignore it. Worse, not following your written policy may provide additional proof of discrimination. It doesn't matter to the law if the alleged harasser is your star employee or the one at the top of the "to-be-fired list." Your policy must be enforced consistently regardless of the identities of the complaining employee and alleged harasser.

E.   Train Your Employees On Appropriate Conduct

All new employees should undergo diversity training to ensure that they understand their legal rights and obligations and the company's policies. Existing employees should have refresher diversity training every two years at minimum, or more frequently if conditions in the workplace make it advisable to do so.

F.   Train Your Supervisors to Respond To Any Complaints

Managers must know a policy exists and how to enforce it. Investigating is part skill and part art. A manager must elicit all the details about the alleged conduct and possible witnesses in an independent and non-judgmental way. Complaining about discrimination in the workplace is difficult. It takes courage to come forward. Employees fear they'll be blackballed if they complain. The interviewer must keep an open mind and have a compassionate ear. Remember, even if the matter doesn't rise to unlawful discrimination, the employee feels very deeply that she's been treated improperly.

Your managers need written procedures to follow if a complaint occurs. Most discrimination isn't overt, and the only witnesses may be the complaining employee and alleged harasser. Managers must be trained to ask the right questions and look for corroborating evidence. If the employee says her supervisor made lewd comments to her on the Williams job site but the company's time records show the two never worked together on that job site, then the evidence contradicts the complaining employee's account. Sometimes corroborating documents like emails containing ethnic slurs will prove one side right. Most of time, the truth is as clear as a bucket of mud.

G.   Document Everything

When interviewing the complaining employee, the alleged harasser or any witnesses, the interviewer must take detailed notes. Get specifics about what was said and done. Review emails and other electronic communications and keep copies of them. Write down the steps you took in your investigation. These records may protect you later if the employee alleges you didn't investigate her claim.

Also, long before a complaint happens your managers should have documented any performance issues for all employees.

Sometimes, an employee with a poor performance track record who is at risk for termination of employment may allege discrimination in an attempt to save his job. This complaint has to be taken just as seriously as any other. But, having a pre-existing, recorded history that documents the performance issues goes a long way toward showing that the reason for the adverse job action (firing, layoff or demotion) was a legitimate business reason (poor performance) and not retaliation for reporting unlawful discrimination.

H.   Take All Complaints Seriously

An employee who sees that you are taking their concerns seriously is less likely to escalate the issue outside the company. These complaints have the potential to seriously damage workplace morale, employee productivity and loyalty as well as the company's reputation and its bottom line. Every complaint is important and must be taken seriously

I.   Consult with an Attorney and Investigate All Complaints

Investigating and responding to a discrimination complaint is not the time to go it alone. Consult with an attorney as soon as a complaint is received.

J.   If the Complaint is Valid, Craft an Appropriate Remedial Response, Which Can Include Transferring or Firing the Harasser

Once the company determines that discrimination or harassment is likely or actually has occurred, it *must* take appropriate remedial steps to stop the harassment and protect the complaining employee. What is appropriate will vary from case to case. Sometimes, reassigning the parties (so long as the victim suffers no loss of status or benefits) and retraining the wrongdoer is a reasonable solution. At other times, reassignment isn't a viable or effective option. If the wrongdoer is a repeat offender or the conduct is significant and serious, then firing the wrongdoer might be the only reasonable response. No employee is so valuable he can't be replaced if he engages in unlawful discrimination or harassment.

K. Let the Person Complaining Know How You Resolved the Complaint

It does a company no good to handle all aspects of a complaint properly but then fail to tell the complaining employee the results of the investigation and what it did to correct the problem. People who complain about discrimination want the bad conduct to stop for them *and* for everyone else who comes after them. They need to know their concerns have been heard and addressed. Not closing the investigational loop with the complaining employee is a huge mistake.

A company, C-Red Inc., received a complaint of inappropriate sex-based comments by a co-worker, Petruchio, from a female employee, Kate. It seems Petruchio was always asking Kate for a kiss. She was also worried about being laid off because C-Red had already reduced everyone's hours. Harassing conduct is unwelcome, and the investigation showed the sexual comments she reported had been made. However, up to the date of her complaint Kate participated in the discussions via text message that she now claimed were "offensive." She'd been sexting (sending explicit sexual photographs) with Petruchio. While the conduct was unacceptable, it didn't rise to legal harassment because it was consensual.

C-Red separated Kate and Petruchio, since changing their job assignments could be done with minimal interruption to the business and no loss of status or benefits for Kate. In addition, Petruchio received a written reprimand, and he and the rest of the supervisory staff went through diversity retraining. C-Red made one mistake. It didn't tell the Kate that Petruchio had received a written reprimand and undergone additional diversity training. The remedial actions worked, and the unprofessional conduct stopped. However, when Kate later resigned, she sued the company, asserting that the company's lack of action on her complaint created a "hostile work environment" that forced her to quit (also known as being "constructively discharged," an additional violation under the anti-harassment laws). Not closing the investigational loop bought the company a lawsuit.

L.   Keep It Confidential

This point may seem to contradict the example I just gave, but it really doesn't. When a company receives a complaint, it must take steps to limit the dissemination of this information to individuals who need to know. There are two primary reasons to keep the complaint and resulting investigation confidential.

First, the company must respect the feelings and reputations of the parties involved. The charge might be unfounded or the misconduct might not rise to legal discrimination. Where there has been unlawful discrimination, the complaining witness shouldn't be the subject of further humiliation, hurt or office gossip.

Second, the company must protect a complaining employee from retaliation. The company's ability to monitor responses becomes more difficult the more people who know about the complaint. The company reduces its risk of a later retaliation claim by limiting the number of individuals with knowledge of the complaint. If a later decision-maker didn't know about the complaint, she can't have retaliated for it when she passed up the complaining employee for a promotion. Only those with a need to know—the alleged victim, alleged harasser, witnesses and key management personnel—should have access to the complaint and related investigation materials.

Even then, the complaining employee must know that complete anonymity or confidentiality can't be guaranteed.

M. Don't Retaliate Against the Person Who Complained

A person complaining about discrimination or harassment (or engaging in several other types of legally protected activity) is protected from retaliation. The company may not take an adverse job action against a complaining employee because he complained. Adverse job actions can include demotion, lateral transfer to a less prestigious position, negative performance reviews, increased performance scrutiny, firing or a host of other actions that put the employee at some disadvantage.

However, a complaining employee is subject to all the company's normal operational and performance requirements. The company need not stop a planned layoff just because an employee makes a harassment complaint.

An employee, Earl, alleged he'd been written up for poor performance, talking on his cell phone during business hours and walking off a job site because he was African American and the company owner, Tom, was Caucasian.

During the investigation process with the EEOC, Earl continued walking off job sites to take personal calls on his cell phone during business hours. Construction Co. wrote him up for violating its written policies and prior warnings. Earl became very upset. At the end of his shift that day, Earl saw Tom in the parking lot, revved his truck's engine and tried to run over Tom. Construction Co. then called me and ultimately fired the employee. The EEOC had no problem finding that the firing was for a legitimate reason rather than wrongful retaliation. But, again, these extremes rarely happen.

Also, if the company finds the complaint was frivolous—had absolutely no merit—it may be able to take appropriate disciplinary actions against the complaining employee. Consult with an attorney when your company must take corrective action or reassign an employee with a current or past complaint of discrimination for any reason.

How to Avoid the Most Common Things Your Employees Do That Can Get You Sued

Employees are a company's greatest asset and weakness. They can strand a company in a legal minefield if policies and procedures aren't in place to protect the company. Managing employees requires:

- Providing scripts for sales employees to use with customers, potential and actual.

- Having written policies covering the main landmines companies can run over.

- Training for your employees and managers on how to recognize, avoid, stop and investigate harassment and discrimination, and how to avoid retaliation.

- Having a retention policy for electronic communications.

- Avoiding the use of third-party materials in the company's business, communications and social media unless you've verified that you may use the material.

- Monitoring your employee's business and personal social media posts.

- Taking all complaints of discrimination or harassment seriously.

- Getting professional advice immediately when these issues arise.

- Creating a trusted advisor network so, when issues arise, you have the resources you need to respond.

A company can't grow unless it has employees. Their actions and inactions can get your company sued. Most of the time, employees make critical mistakes out of ignorance rather than maliciousness. As an employer, you need to establish the policies and procedures to guide your employee's interactions and ensure an ethical and prosperous workplace.

CHAPTER 11

LANDMINE 10: Not Getting Your Just Desserts (Collections)

Don't involuntary donate your service or finance someone else's business. Take steps to ensure you get paid.

t's a cash flow nightmare: You've done the work, sent the invoice to the client and ... crickets. Payment doesn't show up, and your client isn't answering your calls. The business has paid its employees to perform and now isn't sure if it can make the next payroll because its clients are no-pay or slow-pay. Either of those is a disaster for a growing business. When you are in business, a cash flow crunch means that meeting your personal obligations just got that much harder. Not getting paid when you're supposed to puts the business, its employees and its owners in jeopardy.

A profitable technology company, Tech Inc., had a lucrative contract with the federal government. Not surprisingly, the scope of work grew during the project. When this happens, the contractor can request an "equitable adjustment" or change to the contract terms. Tech Inc. made a business decision to wait until closer to the end of the contract to request the adjustment for the extra work. After all, Tech Inc. had great cash flow and had invested in real property, which it could leverage if cash became an issue.

Near the end of the multi-year project, Tech Inc. issued a multi-million-dollar request for equitable adjustment. There were significant delays in processing the adjustment. The company ran out of money to meet payroll and faced termination for default under its other government contracts. In the federal contracting world, being fired for "default" on one contract means that company is barred from any further government contracts. What had seemed to be a good business decision at the time was having horrific repercussions.

Tech Inc. filed bankruptcy to survive while the adjustment, which would be granted at least in part, was being processed. Even that extreme measure wasn't enough. Tech Inc. was forced to sell its real estate holdings to pay off its creditors. When the contract adjustment finally came through and Tech Inc. was paid, the business had ceased operations and the owner had sold many of his personal assets to stay afloat. The significant delay in collection had cost Tech Inc., its employees and its owner everything.

How do you prevent a client's slow-pay or no-pay from shutting down your business?

Have a Written Contract

The first way to ensure your business gets paid for the work it does is to have a good client agreement. I talked about the reasons for having written contracts in Chapter 2 and some specific provisions in Chapter 7. Take a second to look back at those sections before we talk about how contracts can get you paid. I'll wait.

Oh, good. You're back.

A written contract helps you get paid in four ways. As crazy as it sounds, ten thousand or twenty thousand dollars isn't a lot of money to sue over. Don't get me wrong. In real life, ten to twenty thousand dollars is a ton of money. But if you don't have a written contract that allows you to recover your legal fees, the cost of getting a judgment in court and collecting what you are owed may cost you more than the debt itself.

Lipstick Media hired a contractor, Websites R Us, to redevelop its magazine's website for seventy-five hundred dollars. Lipstick had made periodic payments based on promises of completion. Desperate to complete the work, Lipstick hired another consultant to work with the web designer. Still, over a year later, the website wasn't finished or, as far as Lipstick and its new consultant could tell, Websites hadn't even started work yet. Lipstick sued for fifteen thousand dollars—the funds it had paid to Websites plus the consultant's fees. Websites sued (if you can believe it) for ten thousand dollars for the incomplete website. The resulting settlement allowed Lipstick to recover a few thousand dollars above what it cost to sue. To avoid being upside-down because of your litigation expenses, have written agreements with an attorney's fee provision with all your clients.

Written agreements may also lengthen the time you have to sue for the fees the business is owed. If you've ever heard a lawyer advertise on television, radio or the web you know that the law limits the time you have to bring a claim. This is true whether the claim is for a personal injury (the subject of most legal TV advertisements) or collecting for a breach of contract or nonpayment of an invoice. As you can see from the Statute of Limitations Chart in Appendix A at the end of this book, in some states, having a written contract makes a dramatic difference — up to five years—in how long you have to sue.

Another way a good written agreement helps your business collect what is owed is that the agreement narrows the possible areas of dispute. With an oral agreement, the business must prove that an agreement even existed! If the business can't prove that the parties agreed on all the material terms, then it usually can't get paid. A written contract can also limit the defenses y our client might have. The client may argue that it expected certain services for the price, but if your contract says the scope doesn't include those tasks, then that's one defense the client doesn't have.

Get Paid Up Front

A business can help reduce client payment issues by controlling how those payments are structured. When I started my law firm, I fell into the standard billing structure; I issued an invoice at the beginning of the month for work already performed and then waited with fingers crossed, h oping I'd receive payment within the fifteen days our agreement provided. For new clients, I took a deposit against invoices; but the deposits only covered the first month's billings, so after that I was on the same bill and pray cycle.

I was working with a coach who asked me a question that changed everything for the financial health of my business. She asked if there was any reason I had to bill in this manner. The answer was, "Ah, well, no." So, I shifted. Rather than send bills out once a month, I sent out half my bills on the first of the month and the second half on the fifteenth of the month. The change in cash flow pattern allowed me to grow the business and move from a famine to an abundance mindset.

Some of the things you can do to assist with the cash flow waves include, where possible:

- Get a deposit or percentage payment up front. If you work with consumers, your state's consumer protection act might limit the deposit you can take, so check your local law.

- Don't deliver the final product without final payment.

- Send invoices more than once a month if you can. To ease the cash flow crunch, send half of your invoices on the first and the second half on the fifteenth, as my firm did.

- Send invoices on net 10 or 15 rather than net 30 terms. Having a shorter turnaround time for your client's payment means you operate at less risk since you'll know sooner that payment is an issue.

- Have the client's credit card on file and obtain authorization to present a payment five or ten days after the invoice is sent out. If the client is paying a set monthly amount, have her authorize payment of that fee on a specific day of the month and auto-bill the customer's credit card. Remember, if you have the client's financial information you must protect that information and comply with privacy laws.

- Have an out clause so the business doesn't finance the services it provides to its clients. Don't get into a deeper non-payment hole than you have to. Your contract should have a client cutoff point—either a specific number of days late or an overdue amount or a combination of both. My client agreements allow me to stop services once the client is fifteen days past due. By having a specific out clause for non-payment, a business can limit its expenditure of resources on poor-paying clients.

- Communicate with your clients about cost. Surprised clients are unhappy clients, and unhappy clients rarely pay their bills. Be transparent in billings. Answer questions about costs and expenses as they arise.

- Respond to all customer complaints. Again, unhappy clients don't pay their bills. Often, problems that lead to nonpayment can be headed off if the customer's concerns are addressed in a timely manner.

Beware of the Consumer Protection Act

If a business sells to consumers, state consumer protection acts may provide the consumer certain rights, like a three-day recession period or other protections. Violating a consumer protection act may not only invalidate the business's contract but also expose the company to liability for damages, statutory fines and legal fees.

A homeowner, Sorcha, purchased an Angie's List package for a basic kitchen renovation. Sorcha came to Renovate's showroom to pick out materials and substantially upgraded the job. Renovate sent Sorcha a quote crediting her for the special and listing the additions. After a verbal approval for the additional expenses, Renovate started work. But Sorcha didn't pay for the additional services. When the case came to court, Sorach asserted that Renovate had violated Virginia's Consumer Protection Act because the changes and additional costs weren't in writing, and countersued for the money she paid for the Angie's List package and attorney's fees. Renovate didn't get paid for all the additional work it did because it unintentionally violated the Virginia Consumer Protection Act. Be familiar with your state's consumer protection act to prevent unintentional violations.

Understand the Fair Debt Collection Practices Act

Another misunderstood law that affects a business's ability to collect from its client is the Fair Debt Collection Practices Act (FDCPA). This federal law limits what a *third party* can do in collecting a debt. A business can't violate the FDCPA when it seeks to collect its own debt. So, your company's demand for payment isn't limited by, and the client isn't entitled to the procedures and protections of, the FDCPA. If you turn the debt over to a debt collector, however, then the consumer is entitled to the protections of the FDCPA. Debt collectors can include attorneys.

Among other rights, the consumer may dispute the debt and request verification. If the consumer requests verification, all collection actions must stop until that verification is provided. Debt collectors who violate the FDCPA will owe the consumer a minimum of a thousand dollars per violation, plus costs and legal fees. If your business collects debts for others, consult with counsel to ensure you have the proper procedures in place to avoid a FDCPA violation. If your business will use a debt collector, factor in the verification time period and other protections afforded to the consumer and give the collection to the debt collector well before any statute of limitations expires to ensure you have enough time to sue.

Understand the Litigation Process and Hire Competent Counsel

Most state courts have three levels of trial courts. Although the names of the courts change, essentially there's a small claims court, a lower court and a higher court. Small claims are generally limited to claims for money totaling less than five thousand dollars. In many small claims courts, a company can represent itself without counsel. Lower courts also have limits on the size of the claims they can hear. As an example, in Virginia, the General District Court can hear claims of up to twenty-five thousand dollars and any landlord-tenant matter. Companies must be represented by counsel in this court. Finally, the highest-level trial court hears claims above a certain amount (in Virginia that amount is fifteen thousand dollars) and all claims where something other than money is sought. The federal courts can hear cases where the parties are from different states and the amount at issue is over seventy-five thousand dollars, or when the claim arises under federal law.

Unlike television, movies and other depictions of court cases, a trial functions in a very regimented way. There are strict deadlines that if missed may prevent your case from going forward or result in a judgment against your interests. The parties engage in discovery, the process of requesting information through written questions, depositions and requests for documents about the other side's case and defenses. Depending on the court's backlog, a trial in the higher courts can take from a year to over three years. Litigation isn't the time to go it alone.

If you pursue collections against a client, hire competent counsel to do so. I talk more about how to hire counsel in Chapter 13, so I'll only touch on it briefly here. Competence refers to more than just knowledge of the law. Competent trial counsel also knows the local rules that apply to each court, and is able to clearly communicate with you about your case. Because litigation is time-consuming and expensive, your attorney should recommend means other than litigation to resolve the dispute. Understand that settlement requires the consent of all parties and sometimes a case can't be resolved no matter how extraordinary your attorney is.

Litigation should be a last resort. But if you walk into that arena, do so well armed.

How to Avoid Non-payment Landmines

A business's failure to get paid for its work jeopardizes its existence and its owner's financial health. There are many things a company can do to ensure it gets paid for its services.

- If you work with consumers, ensure you aren't unintentionally violating your state's consumer protection law. Even unintentional violations of this law can prevent you from getting paid.

- Leverage your written contracts and policies to your advantage.

- When possible, get paid up front or have the client agree to an automatic payment schedule. When advance payment isn't viable, you can smooth many cash flow bumps by sending half your invoices on the first of the month and the rest on the fifteenth of the month. If you are being paid on a percentage-of-completion basis, negotiate larger payments up front so you can cover your overhead.

- When permissible, don't deliver the final product until payment is full is received.

- If collection actions are inevitable, make sure whoever is collecting the debt for you complies with the FDCPA.

- Understand the litigation process and the time limitations on bringing suit. As you can see from the Statute of Limitations Chart in Appendix A, the time you have to sue varies wildly from state to state and depends on the different claims you have.

- Seek competent legal advice when it comes time to sue. The attorney's fee provision in your written contract will help defray some of the costs of collection and may make settlement more likely.

- Properly manage the billing and payment relationship to ensure you aren't involuntarily donating your services to your clients.

CHAPTER 12

LANDMINE 11: Sabotaging Yourself If You Get Sued or Are Suing Someone

Litigation is never easy, but there are things
you can do to better manage the process.

Y ou might think that, as a lawyer, I don't know what it's like to be on the receiving end of a lawsuit. Sadly, you'd be wrong. Litigation is a cost of doing business regardless of what business you're in.

I'd represented a client for a year before the company hired someone else. While the attorney-client relationship hadn't been wonderful, we'd managed to do good work for the client. The client's bankruptcy matter continued without me. Over the next year, I worked on other matters and changed firms. In other words, life went on for everyone—until I received a notice from the court to appear before it and explain why I shouldn't be held in contempt for allegedly lying to it. I hadn't, but that didn't mean my now-former client and its new attorney couldn't accuse me of doing so. If the allegations were proven to be true, my entire career was in jeopardy. Talk about drag? I was living in it for over four years while the allegations were resolved.

Receiving documents telling you that you've been sued is like getting punched in the gut while all the air is simultaneously sucked out of the room. Trust me; I know. Even knowing that I hadn't done what my former client alleged, I couldn't risk not taking the matter seriously and not aggressively defending myself. After many days of trial, the bankruptcy court found that the allegations of my lying to it were false (although I'd made a mistake in not updating the court on a possible conflict of interest), but I still went through all the highs and lows of litigation as a party and ran up a huge legal bill myself. Four years of drag is a lot whether you're the plaintiff or defendant. It can be crippling. What can you do to minimize the litigation drag?

Well, use the tips from the earlier parts of this book. But when litigation is likely, there are steps you can take to minimize the drag on your business. Just like grieving, there are stages to the litigation process. Once you have recovered from the emotional shock of being sued, you need to take certain steps to protect your business. This is another area where what you don't know can hurt your business and its chances in the litigation.

You're "It"

A lawsuit is started when a defendant is served with a legal document that tells him he's been sued and how long he has to respond to the lawsuit. This document is called a "summons." The initial documents may also include court orders setting up some rules for the case or scheduling an initial hearing. You don't have to accept the summons to be validly served. You don't have to actually get the documents either.

Many states allow "alternate service," meaning the documents don't have to be handed to you in person. Some states allow a defendant to receive the summons by certified mail. If you live outside of the state where the lawsuit is filed, you could be served when the plaintiff sends the summons to a statutory agent and that agent mails you the summons by certified mail. In Virginia, a plaintiff can serve an out-of-state defendant by sending a copy of the lawsuit to the *Virginia* Secretary of the Commonwealth. Service is complete once the Secretary mails the certified letter to the defendant.

In one case, the sheriff posted service at the defendant's home (he literally taped the lawsuit to the front door). The defendant, Kamal, was out of the country for sixty days. Unfortunately for him, the time to respond to a lawsuit in Virginia is only twenty-one days after service. So, by the time Kamal came home, a judgment had been entered against him for his failure to respond to the lawsuit. He asked the court to undo the judgment because he didn't actually get notice of the lawsuit. The court denied his request.

As tempting as it is, trying to ignore the problem won't work; litigation won't just go away. Things will get worse as default judgments are made based on your failure to respond. Time for your initial response is short, and missing deadlines has dire consequences. The time to respond to a lawsuit varies from state to state, and the federal courts have different time limits as well. Once you receive a copy of a lawsuit, you need to take action. Fast.

Initiate a Litigation Hold on Your Documents

You must save anything that might be related to the case as soon as you know a dispute is possible. Once you are likely to sue or be sued, you must put a "litigation hold" on your documents—meaning you need to save everything and protect documents from inadvertently being lost or destroyed. Your employees and IT department must know about the litigation and be told not to delete any information that might be related to it. If your computer system automatically writes over backup copies, you must stop this process and make a copy of everything on the system on the day you found out about the possibility of a lawsuit.

Making copies of the information is expensive and might seem like a waste of resources, but the price of not protecting documents from inadvertent destruction is much higher. If you don't preserve the data, a court may later decide you "spoiled" or destroyed evidence. The court can then make rulings adverse to you because information was accidentally deleted. You might lose your case because you didn't protect this information.

Get All Your Documents Together

Once you've taken steps to protect the information related to the litigation, you need to get it all in one place. Gather all of the relevant documents, letters, emails, contracts, bills, photographs and anything else that has anything to do with the dispute. Emails should be saved as both print and electronic records. Err on the side of including too much. Don't leave anything out.

In the case, you'll be asked for information relevant to the lawsuit. Don't cull information because you don't think it's "relevant," because this term is also legal mumbo jumbo. In litigation, "relevant" means anything that may lead to the discovery of information either side could use. The net is very broad. A document that merely mentions one of the parties might ultimately be important. Let your attorney decide what needs to be turned over to the other side.

Call Your Attorney or Hire One If You Don't Have an Existing Relationship

In an ideal world, you already have a lawyer on speed dial. If not, ask friends, family and trusted advisors for recommendations for an attorney to represent you. Most state bar associations have resources for attorney searches. Check out the websites or blogs of any recommended attorneys and make sure they practice the area of law relevant to your lawsuit.

Interview any recommendation and any attorney you find through an Internet search. Ensure the attorney has experience with your type of dispute. Almost more important than the lawyer's knowledge of the area is ensuring that attorney is a personality fit for you. Your lawyer must complement your business style; you don't want to be at cross-purposes with your lawyer.

Discuss Any Possible Claims Against the Person Suing You with Your Attorney

The law often requires you to assert any claims you have against the person suing you or lose those claims. Never bring a frivolous claim in the hopes it will give you leverage in settling the case, but know there can be strategic advantages to a countersuit. Remember, countersuits will likely increase costs and may make settlement harder rather than easier.

Learn What Deadlines Apply

Once you've been sued, you must respond to the lawsuit within days. The amount of time you have will often depend on where you are sued. The summons, the document telling you about the lawsuit, will say when you need to file a response with the court and plaintiff. If you are unsure about deadlines, ask your attorney or any attorney you are interviewing to represent you.

Whether you are the plaintiff or defendant, other deadlines will apply once the litigation starts. Each side will seek information from the other side, and motions (documents asking the court to take certain actions) will be filed. Your court's rules will set forth how quickly you have to act. Not responding within the required time period can cause adverse rulings and sanctions (or punishment) for not complying with the deadlines.

Your attorney can't do her job in a timely manner or protect you to the best of her ability if you aren't meeting the deadlines she sets. Make sure any deadline, whether court- or attorney-imposed, is scheduled on your calendar.

Get Access to Money

Litigation is expensive. Even a small case can cost thousands of dollars to prosecute or defend. Courts publish guidelines on reasonable legal fees in their area. A brand-new lawyer with less than three years of experience can cost you $275 per hour. A lawyer with twenty or more years of experience can cost $820 per hour or more. Your attorney can give you an estimate on how much the case might cost you.

If you can't pay to litigate a case, be up front with your attorney. There's nothing worse (for you or your attorney) then getting into a case and having your attorney quit in the middle because you can't pay him. If you can't afford to litigate the matter, your attorney should work to resolve the dispute, if possible, rather than fight it.

Sometimes, a lawyer will prosecute a case (sue someone else) on a contingency basis, in which the lawyer doesn't get paid unless you recover money, but don't count on finding someone who will take your case on this basis. A lawyer may take a case on a contingency basis when liability is likely and the other side has the apparent ability to pay. Common contingency-amenable cases are car accidents or other claims where the defendant has insurance. In those cases, the lawyer knows that, if his client obtains a judgment, the insurance company is likely to pay the amount due. Contingency cases are also a bulk business. An attorney who accepts contingency matters will handle many cases that don't pay at all for every contingent case that pays her well. It's highly unlikely you'll find a lawyer to *defend* a case on a contingency basis when you have no claims against the person suing you.

Sometimes an attorney will offer to take the case on a *pro bono* basis (without charge to you). Again, don't count on this. Remember, we're running businesses, too. We can't afford to take every case for every client that can't pay us. I've had to pass on cases that needed to be litigated because the economics of taking the case didn't make sense for my business.

A word of caution about attorney's fees and awards. If your contract or a law allows you to recover reasonable legal fees, remember the key words are "recover" and "reasonable." Most times you will have to pay your attorney as the case progresses, so any award will serve as reimbursement of those fees rather than payment. A court will only grant you reasonable legal fees. You can hire an attorney that costs a thousand dollars an hour (I know one opposing counsel who charges that rate), but don't assume the court will allow you to recover a thousand dollars an hour for his time. A court will determine an attorney's reasonable billing rate based on his years of experience and the area's prevailing rates. The court could find that the reasonable rate for your thousand-dollar-an-hour attorney was only six hundred dollars per hour. You would still owe the other four hundred dollars per hour to your attorney.

Besides looking at whether the lawyer's billing rate was reasonable, the court will consider whether the time the lawyer spent on your matter was reasonable. I had one case where the other side filed a simple motion to compel discovery against my client, Ahab, because he missed the production deadline. To dissuade parties from stonewalling the discovery and litigation process, the court's rules strongly favor an award of the other side's legal fees when there's a dispute over what information must be provided. The motion should have taken only an hour to prepare. Yet the other side argued they'd spent over eighty hours working on this simple motion! Their initial demand to resolve the dispute was for my client to pay a hundred thousand dollars in legal fees. The time spent on the motion was shocking. We settled the sanctions issue for Ahab's failure to respond in a timely fashion to discovery for a lot less than one hundred thousand dollars, Even assuming the other firm had spent all eighty hours working on the motion it was likely that if the court had to decide the matter, it would only enter a small award based on what it believed was a reasonable amount of time to spend on the motion. Finally, if you assert several claims and only win on some of them, the court will apportion you fees between those the claims you won or lost. So, while you may spend one hundred thousand dollars on the litigation, the court may only award a fraction of that amount.

Take my advice: Don't litigate or set your litigation strategy because you expect the other side to pay your legal fees. Your legal fee award might bear no resemblance to the legal fees you paid.

Try to Settle

Most cases don't go to trial. Settlement allows the parties to get creative in resolving the dispute. The law often prevents the other side from using your settlement offer as proof you owe them. The reality is, once you walk into a courtroom your odds of "winning" are only fifty-fifty no matter how good your case looks on paper. Whether you're the plaintiff or defendant, settlement saves you the time and expense of litigation and gives you certainty. If you owe the other side, you can often negotiate payment terms that allow your business to keep running and avoid bankruptcy.

Keep your expectations reasonable. Litigation will take longer, cost more and cause more stress than you imagine. Most people don't have million-dollar claims. If the plaintiff's or your counterclaims' best-case scenario is recovering a hundred thousand dollars, realize that a good settlement may be as little as twenty-five thousand dollars, depending on the cost to litigate and the likelihood of success.

A lawyer will handicap your claim.

Handicapping a horse is giving the odds of winning. What is "handicapping a claim"?

It's assessing the viability of your different courses of actions and possible results. A good lawyer helps you evaluate the pros and cons and the costs and benefits of your claims, any counterclaims and both sides' defenses. Sometimes a claim that seems viable isn't actually worth pursuing. But you won't know that until a handicapping analysis is done.

When I'm representing the defendant, and assessing the viability of a claim or settlement option, I consider factors that may surprise you. What's the first thing I estimate? The cost of the dispute, in hard cash and lost opportunity costs. Factors for this include: existence or lack of an attorneys' fee provision, the litigation budget, the time commitment, the company's ability to bear the expense of litigation, the possible judgment amount and the likelihood of collecting that judgment. Client expectations are also a factor. TV and movies make people think all claims are million-dollar claims. They aren't.

I also consider non-monetary risks like the possibility of counter-claims, the difficulty in proving certain types of claims like fraud, the believability and likability of the witnesses, the judge assigned, the strength of the claim, the time it will take to get to trial and resulting lost business opportunities for my client, the facts and other less tangible issues. From those factors, I'll develop a number representing the cost or risk associated with the case. Then I'll subtract this number from my client's possible best case recovery and reduce that product by another ten percent to account for the unknown.

These factors are on a sliding scale, and handicapping a case is as much art as it is accounting. If there's a concern that the legal fees might be more than you can win in court, you need to know up front. In that case, aggressive settlement negotiation makes more sense than a drive to litigation. Or you might have a very strong case and a financially weak defendant. Though some litigate for the principle of the thing, clients are rarely happy with a Pyrrhic victory. When the defendant has few collectable assets, weigh the expense of getting a paper judgment heavily against the loss from not pursuing the claim.

Did you notice the facts came in nearly last in my calculation?

There's a reason for that. The first factors balance the cost against the benefit of litigation; the facts can be used to calculate a percentage for your chance of recovery. Juries make mistakes. Courts make mistakes. If the court refuses to let in evidence that is critical to your case because it makes a bad call, you might lose a case that, on paper, you should have won. Juries are swayed to some extent by how likable the parties are. The human factor in litigation can't be underestimated.

Accepting or rejecting a settlement is *always* the client's decision. Try to look at a settlement offer (whether you are receiving or making one) as a business decision. Understand that if a lawyer is recommending you make or accept a twenty-five thousand-dollar settlement offer on a hundred thousand-dollar claim, there's a reason for it. Ask your lawyer to explain the basis for his recommendation.

Be Wary of Litigating for the "Principle"

Lawyers have a love-hate relationship with clients who sue or refuse to settle over the "principle." These cases last longer and cost more than cases where reasonable business judgment prevails. This is good for the lawyer, since he's likely to earn a larger fee. But people who litigate over principles are more likely to be unhappy with the results—and final costs.

Whether you're the plaintiff or defendant, don't sue (or countersue, as the defendant) unless you have a solid case and the economics of litigation make sense. Unfortunately, some good claims are simply too expensive to bring. Most states have lower courts that handle smaller claims (usually up to twenty-five thousand dollars) and a higher court for cases with larger claims or specific types of remedies. Unless you have a contract that allows you to recover your legal fees, most of the time you must pay your own lawyer. If your company is the party to the lawsuit, it must be represented by an attorney. There are cases that *must* be brought in the higher court that aren't cost-effective to bring. Before litigating, step back and see if the suit (either filing or defending it) makes economic sense.

If you're litigating over hard feelings or for the principle, whether as the plaintiff or defendant, consider finding someone to vent to. A therapist is much less expensive than a lawsuit, and you'll probably feel better too.

Don't Make Your Attorney's Job Harder

Your attorney can't represent your interests without your help. It's tempting to think your job is done once you hire an attorney. Let me tell you a secret. It's not.

Your primary duty as a client is to give your attorney any information she asks for. Remember Ahab, the client I said had to pay a discovery sanction earlier in this chapter? That happened because the court's time limits were short and Ahab wanted to save on legal fees, so he didn't send me the documents until the last minute. The clock ran out, and Ahab was left without a seat after the buzzer. The information you send your attorney is raw data. Your attorney must review it, compare it to the information requested and decide if the document is relevant. If it is relevant, the document must then be marked for production by Bates stamping, that is, have an identifying number placed on it. This takes time, especially when there are a lot of documents.

Ahab wanted to save money, but in the end paid much more than he would have had he given me the documents at the start of the case. Why? In addition to the sanctions award Ahab paid, I had to hire extra people to review over forty thousand documents in a week. The expense for the temporary help was one Ahab had to bear. Withholding the documents from his attorney was a very costly mistake.

Another costly mistake clients make is not telling the lawyer the full story. Sometimes a client will gloss over information because he's embarrassed or thinks the other side won't find the smoking gun. Trust me. The other side *will* find the information you don't want them to see. Your lawyer can't give you the best advice possible if she doesn't know all the facts. Sometimes damaging information can be managed if the lawyer knows about it *before* the testimony comes out in court. If the information is truly devastating to your case, you want your lawyer to know as soon as possible. There's nothing I hate more than watching a strong case get flushed down the tubes because I was denied vital, need-to-know information. I've been able to settle bad cases earlier and less expensively—*before* the other side learned of the weaknesses in the client's case or defense— when I knew there was a problem at the start.

Don't overly restrict your lawyer's options or strategy choices. You hire a lawyer because we have experience in handling your matter, whether in litigation or not. At times, a client's desire to save legal expenses will make protecting that client's interests nearly impossible. In one case, a client's desire to limit her legal fees on its very strong case with the right to recover legal fees caused her to issue instructions like:

- Don't discuss this matter with another lawyer in the firm who is handling a related matter.

- Send the email they drafted and sent to me, with comments that would be otherwise protected under the attorney-client privilege, directly to opposing counsel without editing.

- Don't email them with my concerns about their course of action, because they won't pay for that time.

- Accept terms in a potential settlement agreement that are probably unenforceable rather than spend the time to negotiate the provision to make it enforceable.

The client had hamstrung my ability to counsel them and represent their interests. I ultimately ended that attorney-client relationship even though the client paid her bill on time every month. Why?

I could not achieve the client's goals with my hands tied behind my back and a gag shoved in my mouth. Talking to the client, who was no longer listening to my advice, was frustrating. To protect my firm from a later malpractice claim, I was spending time documenting how she was acting against my advice. In the end, it was better to terminate the relationship than represent a client I could not protect from itself.

If you don't hear from your attorney for a while during active litigation, please call to get a status update. But don't call every day. Calling every day gets expensive. Lawyers bill on tenth-of-an-hour, or six-minute, increments. Many lawyers have minimum charges: for a phone call it's usually a quarter or three-tenths of an hour and for an email usually a tenth of an hour, because while your call may only last eight minutes, the disruption to the workflow is closer to fifteen to twenty minutes as the lawyer changes gears and writes notes about your call. Those increments add up. Instead of calling for reports, trust that your attorney will tell you about important developments as they happen.

You are paying your lawyer to advise you. Don't reject that advice out of hand. One client, Marlin, often called to ask questions with preferred answers in mind. The conversation went, "Can I do *this*?" He wanted a "yes." When he got a "no" instead, he'd hang up the phone and call the partner who worked on the case to ask the same question. Marlin was fishing for a different answer. The pattern was so predictable that when I hung up the phone with Marlin, I could walk down the hall to the partner's office and have just enough time to tell him what happened before Marlin client was on the partner's line. If Marlin still didn't get the answer he wanted, he usually did what we recommended against anyway. Down the road, he'd call back and say, "Remember when you told me not to do *this*? Well, I did it. Now I need help undoing it." The firm earned lots of money fixing the problems Marlin created by not listening to our advice. But he was frustrating to work with. And ultimately, he made a mistake we couldn't correct and lost his business. I've fired clients who routinely wouldn't listen to my advice.

It's okay to disagree with your lawyer or not take her advice. Getting a second opinion is fine too. But have a good reason not to follow the advice you've been given.

Get Ready for Trial

While some courts can hear a case within a year from filing, most average closer to three years to resolve a dispute. Realize this is a marathon and not a sprint. Though most cases settle before trial, don't assume yours will. From the start, you need to prepare as if you are going to trial. Clear your schedule of major obligations so you can assist your attorney. Don't tie your lawyer's hands in preparing the case to avoid expenses in the hope that the matter will settle. Discovery, the process of getting information from the other side about their case, is only available for a limited period of time. Delaying the start of this process will likely result in a mad scramble to get your case ready. Mad scrambles are expensive, as your lawyer may need to hire temporary help to meet short deadlines. Being ready to go to trial helps your settlement position.

Forget *Perry Mason*—or any Other Trial Show or Movie You've Watched

Law shows make trials much more exciting than they really are. Perry Mason always had a surprise witness or could destroy an adverse witness on the stand with new evidence. This rarely — read as almost never—happens in real trial work. In civil cases, the only evidence used at trial has been disclosed to the other side during the pre-trial or discovery phase. Late-produced evidence that unfairly surprises the other side is rarely admitted.

A show compresses months of work and days of trial so all you see are the exciting bits. That's not to say there aren't exciting bits or devastating cross-examinations of witnesses, but those aren't the norm. Oh, and remember that reality court shows like *Judge Judy* are as much about entertainment as they are about the law.

Science and technology aren't as advanced as they are shown to be on television. DNA reports take months to obtain rather than hours. Many of the magic gizmos in crime dramas don't exist yet. Juries, so used to crime dramas, may unfairly judge one side for not having impossible technology.

Another misconception entertaining legal shows perpetuate is that a jury comprises twelve people. This isn't always true outside a criminal case. In many states or federal courts, your case may be decided by nine or even six people. Sometimes a jury may not have to reach a unanimous decision.

Trial work is tedious and requires exhaustive preparation. Even then, it's impossible to predict everything that will happen at trial. Just don't judge your case by what you've seen in some show. Please.

Seek A Friendly Shoulder

Litigation is stressful. Attorneys are called "counselors at law" for a reason. At least half my time is spent listening to my clients' concerns and advising them about how to react. If you are in litigation, you need an emotional sounding board outside your attorney.

Have I scared you to death? Well, now for the ray of light.

I enjoy litigating cases. I'm not afraid of going into a courtroom and fighting it out. No litigator I know who stays in this profession for long is scared. But the bottom line is: My job as an attorney isn't to win at all costs. My job is to make your problems go away as quickly and inexpensively as possible. If we cross the court's threshold, you've already lost to some degree, even if it's just time spent away from running your business. Making the problem go away often means settling a case. Lucky for you, the other side knows this too. Depending on who's reporting, you'll find statistics saying that as few as three percent to as many as twelve percent of cases filed go to trial. Our job, as lawyers, is to get the best deal possible. If everyone is being reasonable, your case will be resolved before trial either through rulings made by the court before trial or through settlement.

Just because the goal is settlement doesn't mean you have to roll over. A strong case, whether as plaintiff or defendant, will drive the settlement value. Some key settlement windows are early in the case before either side has spent too much on legal fees or after the court makes a critical ruling. Always evaluate your settlement position based on the realities of your case and the rulings made in it.

Oh. And one more point: Though settlement favors the plaintiff, court doesn't. Plaintiffs lose about half the time. So, whether you are suing or being sued really doesn't count for much when it comes to predicting the outcome of a settlement or case.

How to Avoid Sabotaging Yourself When You Get Sued

- Understand that you don't have to physically accept the legal paperwork to be sued.

- Preserve all documents that might related to the dispute.

- Get all your documents together.

- Call your attorney or hire one.

- Discuss all possible claims you might have against the other side with your attorney to determine if you have grounds for a counter-claim.

- Learn what deadlines apply to avoid default judgments and other negative events.

- Get access to money.

- Try to settle.

- Don't litigate for the principle of the thing.

- Cooperate with your attorney.

- Get ready for trial, a multi-month process.

- Seek a friendly shoulder.

CHAPTER 13

LANDMINE 12: Working with the Wrong Attorney

Did you hear the one that says changing lawyers is like changing deck chairs on the Titanic? Yeah, the attorney-client relationship shouldn't be like that.

You've decided that you need to retain an attorney for your business. But how do you hire one?

You need to consider two factors in hiring an attorney: experience in the area of law you need and "fit." Not all lawyers are created equal. Not all lawyers practice all kinds of law. If you have a business dispute, you need a business lawyer, not a divorce lawyer. Most lawyers confine their practice to a specific niche in the law. Before you hire an attorney, make sure they practice the type of law you need. While general practitioners, lawyers whose practices cover many areas of the law, still exist, they are becoming a dying breed. Like every other business, lawyers are specializing.

If you don't know any lawyers, ask other business owners you work with about their legal counsel. If they won't tell or don't have a regular lawyer, there are resources for finding a lawyer. Whether you find your prospective counsel from a referral or through networking or an Internet search, interview her just as you would an employee. Besides general competence, you need to ensure the attorney's personality and case approach fit with yours. Ideally, you hire a lawyer who is as aggressive or conservative in his work as you are in your approach to life.

I've turned down potential clients or fired existing clients when they wanted me to take a position that didn't mesh with my beliefs or ethics. For example, a prospective client wanted an attorney who would fight every request from the other side no matter how reasonable the request was. The prospective client had a losing case and didn't want to settle. He just wanted to cost the other side as much as possible along the way. This isn't how I litigate.

I firmly believe that all cases can be resolved short of trial if all parties (and their attorneys) act like reasonable business people. Sadly, this doesn't always happen; but most cases settle. When a client has a losing case, I will advocate strongly that she try to resolve the matter rather than incur the expense of litigation. If you want a scorched-earth attorney, you need to hire one; otherwise both you and your attorney will be unhappy working together. Remember, your lawyer will be with you during some of the best and worst times in your life, and you should feel comfortable talking to him.

A lawyer should not get offended when you ask about her experience or how she's handled similar issues for other clients. There are questions you can and should ask any lawyer before you decide whom to hire. Just remember, the interview isn't the time to fish for free legal advice, but to determine if the lawyer has the qualifications you need and is a good fit.

Interview questions fall into four categories: experience, fees, case management and case evaluation. The lists below don't include everything you might want to ask, but should point you in the right direction.

Experience

Generally speaking, you don't want to be your attorney's first client and you don't want your case to be the first time he's handled a similar matter. If you hire an attorney with little experience with your issue who may charge a lower rate as a result, clarify how much of his work involves becoming competent and what is part is involved in representing you.

1. How long has the attorney been in practice?
2. In which jurisdictions or states or courts?
    - Have you appeared in the court where the case is being heard?
3. Have you handled this type of case or issue?
    - What percentage of your caseload comprises similar matters?
    - Are there any issues in this case that you haven't handled?
    - Who is your typical client?
4. Describe your experience in handling cases like mine.
    - How much of that experience was in the last two years?
    - What were the outcomes?
    - What percentage of your cases settled and what percentage have gone to trial?

- What percentage of trials have you won in those cases?

Okay, I don't keep tabs on my win record. So, don't be surprised if the lawyer you're talking to doesn't know. Also, remember that past results do not predict future success. Every case is unique and the result will depend on many factors.

5. What's your current caseload?

- Do you have large trials scheduled over the next few months?
- How many active cases and clients do you work with at one time?

If your matter is urgent and time-consuming, hiring a lawyer who is about to start a three-week trial is not apt to be the right choice.

6. Do you have malpractice insurance? (If the lawyer says "no," run away.)
7. Are you certified by any organization as a specialist or expert in this area?

Most bar associations, which are the administrative agencies that license and supervise attorney conduct, prohibit a lawyer from claiming to be an expert unless a recognized third-party organization has certified them. There aren't many organizations who certify lawyers. As a result, don't be surprised if your lawyer doesn't have any certifications beyond his law degree.

8. Have you ever been sanctioned for misconduct?

If the answer is yes, ask questions until you drill down to the basis for the misconduct claim and the resulting disciplinary action.

9. Can you provide references from other clients?

This is a tricky question for lawyers. We must keep our clients' confidences and secrets. This includes not disclosing who they are. Asking clients for references is a relatively new trend, and not all attorneys are comfortable asking clients for references.

Once you've decided to hire the attorney, or are close to that decision, it's important to ask her how she views your matter.

Case Management and Communication

More legal malpractice claims arise out of an attorney's failure to respond to client inquiries in a timely way than from any other. It's important to know the lawyer's policies on communication and other timeliness issues before you hire him.

1. How long will the matter take?

Clients almost always underestimate how long a matter will take to resolve. Litigation can take years. Even something as apparently simple as writing up a contract might take weeks depending on the number of revisions the document goes through. Getting a reasonable estimate of the time your matter may take to resolve will prevent later frustration on all sides.

2. How will we communicate?

I ask clients this question. When I started practicing law there were only three commonly used options for communications: phone, in person and this newfangled thingy called a facsimile or fax. Now we have more choices. Most clients prefer emails over calls since emails are theoretically less disruptive to one's day. Find out your lawyer's preferred method of communication and let her know yours.

Also, find out how quickly the lawyer will respond to a communication. Most strive to respond within twenty-four hours. But remember, the lawyer won't always make the twenty - four-hour turnaround.

3.   Who will handle my matter?

Law firms have many attorneys, from partners to associates. Most firms will assign your matter to an associate with partner supervision. Sometimes, working only with the partner is important or advantageous, but not always. Also, having an associate or paralegal work on the matter will lower your legal fees.

4.   What would my responsibilities be?
   -    Are there things I can do to improve my situation?
5.   Are there deadlines I should know about?
6.   Will I get copies of all letters, emails, faxes, legal papers and other documents in my case?

You should. If the lawyer says no, he's waving a red flag at you. Run away.

7.   If you do not have the expertise to handle my case on your own, do you work with other lawyers?
   -    Under what circumstances would you allow them to take over the case?
   -    In what circumstances would you refer me to someone else?
8.   How do you resolve complaints?
   -    How do I end this relationship if I'm dissatisfied?
   -    Have you ever fired a client? Why?

Case Evaluation

Asking questions about the specifics of your case before you hire an attorney is an important part of the vetting process. However, remember that the attorney gets paid for his opinion and advice. Don't expect an in-depth analysis during a complimentary consultation. The attorney will generally only share his detailed handicapping of the case and case strategy with you once you've hired him. Issue spotting, or an identification of the main issues your matter presents, is likely the best response you'll get before you commit to hiring the attorney. Here are a few questions you might consider:

1.   What are the possible outcomes?
2.   What strategy would you propose and why?
3.   What alternatives to trial are there?

Fees and Cost Arrangements

1.   Is there a fee for the first consultation, and, if so, how much is it?
2.   How much do you charge in cases like mine?

There are multiple financial options for working with an attorney. These are: pro bono, contingent fees, hourly billing, project or flat fee, blended rates and retainer.

A lawyer represents a client on a pro bono basis when he takes the case on without compensation for his time or solely in anticipation of a later legal fees award. The client always remains responsible for costs of the representation. Very few cases are accepted on this basis. Some legal aid societies will assist indigent individuals on a pro bono basis for certain types of cases. Sometimes a larger firm also has pro bono sections.

A *contingent fee*, when a lawyer agrees to take a percentage of a final award if you win and only costs if you don't, is another example of the lawyer accepting the risk of litigation along with his client. Personal injury claims in which an insurance company is involved are often good prospects for a contingent fee. What motivates an attorney to take these matters is the likelihood of being able to collect the judgment or settlement at the end.

Most lawyers bill on an *hourly* basis. In this arrangement, the lawyer has a set hourly rate, and the client is billed for the actual hours worked using tenth-of-an-hour increments. Paralegals, associates and partners all bill at different hourly rates based on their years of experience.

An alternative to hourly billing is a *flat fee* or *project rate*. The lawyer charges a set price for a specific product or task. Discrete issues such as creating employee handbooks, contracts or the like often work well with this type of arrangement.

Sometimes an attorney will take a litigation matter on *blended rate*, meaning he accepts a lower hourly rate than normal but receives either a percentage of the recovery or an enhanced rate upon success.

For example, an attorney normally charges $425 per hour. A potential client asks the attorney to take a case where liability is likely (the defendant probably did something wrong), but it's unclear whether the defendant has the money to pay a judgment. Lawyer and client may agree to a blended rate arrangement by which the attorney gets paid $225 per hour as the case progresses and a "success fee" of an additional $300 per hour. If they win and collect on the judgment, the attorney's effective hourly rate will be $525 rather than her usual $425. But if they lose the case or win but can't collect the money, the attorney still gets $225 per hour. The higher success rate compensates the attorney for the risk and delay in payment. The client benefits because he gets a significantly reduced fee if he doesn't win.

Most people, including lawyers, misuse the term "retainer." Often, it is misused to mean "legal fee deposit." However, a true retainer is a monthly or annual fee to keep an attorney available for your matters. If you have a lot of legal issues, then this arrangement might work for you.

3. How many hours do you think my case will take?

    - How much do you estimate the matter will cost me?

4. Do you have a minimum unit of time for which you bill?

Most lawyers bill in tenth-of-an-hour increments, but sometimes they have minimum charges for phone calls or emails. Check to see if the firm has a policy on this issue.

5. Will our fee agreement be in writing?

This answer should be "yes." Some bar associations require written fee agreements, but not all of them. Even when a written agreement isn't required, you still want the contract in writing to ensure there are no later misunderstandings.

6. Are expenses extra, and, if so, what expenses do you anticipate?

Expenses, or costs, are almost always extra. What the lawyer considers a cost that should be passed on to the client may vary. As an example, my first firm charged a dollar per page for a fax, whether incoming or outgoing. My current firm does not.

7. How can I reduce the costs?

8. Do I have to pay a deposit?
   - If so, how much?
   - How will you bill against the deposit?
   - What happens when the deposit is used up?
9. How often will I be billed?

Most of the time you will be billed monthly; some bar associations require monthly billing. However, if yours is a contingent fee matter, you might not be billed every month.

10. What happens if I get behind on payments?

Generally, a lawyer has the right, after notice to you, to quit if you don't pay your legal bills in a timely manner. If there is litigation, a lawyer must also ask the court's permission to quit. On some fairly rare occasions, a court may not let your lawyer quit because letting him do so would be unfairly prejudicial to you, such was when trial is coming up soon and you don't have enough time to get another attorney. In trial, the potential harm to the client of the attorney quitting may outweigh the lawyer's financial hardship of staying in the case.

What You Should Expect from Us

Attorneys have a fiduciary duty toward their client. This means we aren't allowed to take action that's against your best interests. Lawyer communication, competency, ethics and fees are important aspects of an attorney-client relationship. You can expect your lawyer to:

A.   Maintain the Attorney-Client Privilege

What you tell your attorney is privileged, which means that the lawyer must keep your secrets, with some narrow exceptions.

Disclosure of the intent to commit a crime is never privileged, and you may forfeit the privilege if you use the lawyer's advice for fraudulent purposes. Also, if the disclosure is made in front of someone who has no duty of confidentiality, like a fact witness or using a public or employer-owned email system, then no privilege exists. Finally, you can't use the privilege to prevent the attorney from testifying about something you told her in a dispute between the attorney and you. Outside of these narrow exceptions, a lawyer can't disclose information you told the lawyer without your permission.

B.   Avoid Conflicts of Interest

The law believes a person cannot serve two masters. A conflict of interest arises when a lawyer has a duty to more than one person or company and the interests of those two people or companies are divergent, or the interests of one could negatively affect the interests of the other. As an example, the lawyer drafts an employee contract for a company. Years later, a company employee consults with the attorney about the contract. The attorney can't represent the employee without violating his duty to the company. A conflict of interest exists and sometimes may prevent the lawyer from representing either the company *or* the employee in their dispute with each other.

C.   Be Competent.

A lawyer should have experience in the area of law she represents you in *or* she should become competent in that area of the law by affiliating with someone with experience or learning the area of law with no charge to you for her education.

D. Educate You About the Law That Applies to Your Situation, Explain How It Affects You or Your Case and Offer Advice

This is the heart of why you hire a lawyer. It's our job to ensure you understand the legal issues that apply to your situation and how you can address them. We also give you the information you need to make good decisions and explain the risks of your possible courses of action. Clients often think it's odd when, after our consultation, I tell them their options include doing nothing. The client always has the option of doing nothing, but this is rarely the best option. Still, I go over what could happen if they ignore the problem so they have the information to weigh the risks and benefits of doing nothing against taking action.

E. Keep You Informed About Your Case

You are entitled to know what's happening in your case, including any changes, delays or setbacks. You can request a regular status report even if that report is "Nothing new is happening" or "We haven't heard back yet about your offer."

F. Acknowledge That Only You Can Make the Important Decisions Regarding Your Case

Trial strategy, which witness to call, which arguments to make, all these fall within the lawyer's discretion. However, important decisions like the scope and objectives of the representation, whether to retain an expert witness (someone with specialized knowledge to support your case or undermine the other side's case), ultimate strategy and whether to settle belong *solely* to the client. Even when the lawyer has discretion, she should (and under many ethics rules has the duty to) consult with you about the strategy to obtain the objectives you set.

G. **File all required documents and pleadings in a timely manner**

H. **Prepare you for your case, including deposition and trial preparation.**

I. **Disclose all fees and costs incurred and charged.**

J. **Admit when we make a mistake.**

All the lawyer jokes aside, we are human and sometimes we mess up. Another case might have blown up and we failed to make a call to opposing counsel to discuss an issue when we said we would. As with most mistakes, often repercussions, if any, are minor and fixable. Whether the mistake is little or the basis for a malpractice claim, we have a duty to tell you about them. Those calls aren't fun for anyone, but they are necessary. It's uncomfortable to admit when a client calls that you forgot to follow up on something, but the client has the right to know and we have the duty to tell.

What You Can't Expect of Your Lawyer

There are some things you can't expect your lawyer to do. Your lawyer will not:

A. **Handle Any Matter He Hasn't Specifically Agreed To**

B. **Guarantee Results or Answer All Questions With a Yes or No**

Clients hate when they ask a question and the lawyer responds, "It depends." Lawyers often express opinions about how they expect things to happen or work out. But there are a lot of factors we can't anticipate or control, such as how a judge will rule on an evidence issue or whether the jury will like or believe a witness. An opinion isn't a guarantee. Ask any trial lawyer who has had more than a dozen cases—we win some we should lose and lose some we should win.

C. Take Any Action Not Allowed by Law or Her Code of Ethics

We all love movies or shows where the bad lawyer is engaged in all sorts of shady and illegal activity. Real life doesn't work this way. Don't expect a lawyer to help break the law or violate her code of ethics.

D. Take an Unreasonable Position Just to Force the Other Side to Incur More Expense or File Any Pleading to Harass or Intimidate the Other Side

The Rules of Professional Conduct (a lawyer's code of ethics, and no, that's not an oxymoron) and state and federal court rules prevent a lawyer from taking a position, filing a document with the court (a pleading) or making an argument in order to harass, intimidate or unreasonably drive up the expense of litigation. A lawyer certifies to a court that the actions she takes are solidly based in the facts or law or make a good faith argument for a change to the law. If a lawyer violates this, she puts her client and herself at risk for sanctions including awards of legal fees and disciplinary action.

What Your Lawyer Should Expect from You

Hiring a lawyer also creates a few responsibilities for you as a client. As a client, your lawyer can expect you to:

A. **Abide by the Agreements You Sign**
B. **Gather All Useful Evidence and Prepare a Summary of Events**
C. **Tell Us Everything and Don't Shade the Facts**

It is a horrible feeling to learn there was a critical piece of information your client didn't tell you, and now the case you thought you had is gone. We can't protect your interests unless you tell us everything (there are caveats to this in criminal law where the lawyer probably won't ask for the client's version of the facts). If the news is bad, the lawyer can help mitigate the damage *if* she knows about it early in the representation. If the news is horrible, the lawyer can help you settle the dispute in the quickest and least expensive manner possible.

D. **Respect Our Time and Schedule**

Someone once said that to a lawyer, a week feels like a day, while to the client a day feels like a week. Most lawyers are aware of the stress their clients are under, especially when litigation is involved. But try to remember we have other cases and lives too.

Back when email first became a major way to communicate, I had to put a disclosure in my representation letter and email auto-responder to the effect that just because you can email me 24/7 does not mean I have the obligation to respond to that email at 11:30 p.m. on a Saturday or 4:00 a.m. Sunday. I had one client who emailed me at 9:00 p.m. Friday, 7:00 a.m. Saturday, 4:30 p.m. Saturday and 4:00 p.m. Sunday about some case issues. I looked at the emails over the weekend, but nothing was urgent or needed to be addressed before Monday. However, Monday morning at 7:30 a.m. I received a "nastygram" via email from the client, accusing me of ignoring him. I had to remind him that he'd emailed me over the weekend and I'd responded in less than one business day. He apologized, and life went on.

We'll do our best to get back to you as soon as possible and treat you as if you were our only client, but sometimes a trial schedule, weekend or vacation may delay the response more than you'd like. So please bear with us.

E. Tell Us When You Won't Be Available

If you are traveling or having surgery and can't assist with your case for a period of time, please let us know. Some issues are time-sensitive. We can often get extensions of deadlines if you aren't available, but we need to know so we can ask.

F. Reply to Requests From Your Attorney in a Timely Manner

Just like when you contact us and expect a timely response, we expect the same. Certain decisions can't be made without you, and deadlines may be tight. Try to get back to us within a business day when you can.

G. Pay Your Bills On Time

Law is a business. Your lawyer has employees and overhead. Pay your lawyer as you pay any other vendor. Talk to your attorney if you run into difficulty paying your bill or think you might. Be proactive. Most of us will work with you on a payment schedule.

When the Lawyer Makes a Mistake

Unfortunately, sometimes lawyers make mistakes. Lawyers carry malpractice insurance, and state bar associations have client recovery funds to assist clients when the attorney doesn't have the required malpractice insurance. Not every mistake is malpractice, though. Malpractice, literally "bad practice," occurs when the lawyer makes a mistake that materially harms the client. Serving requests to have the other side produce documents a week after you promised the client you'd do it is unlikely to rise to malpractice. To win a malpractice claim, the client must show for instance that, but for the lawyer's mistake, the client would have won his lawsuit or not been damaged by a bad contract provision. The client must prove the case within the case.

One lawyer, Phil, was representing the estate of a deceased client in a medical malpractice and wrongful death action for failure to diagnose. Phil had the *original* X-rays showing the doctors should have discovered the client's cancer before it progressed to where it couldn't be treated and caused the client's death. No copies of the X-rays existed. In preparing for trial Phil had the file, including the X-rays, all over his office. His cleaning staff threw the X-rays out. Phil had failed to secure the client's property, which is an ethical violation, and without the X-rays his client lost. Even though losing the X-rays was clearly negligent, the client still had to prove that the estate would have won the original case if the X-rays still existed.

Often there is an ethics violation as well as a malpractice claim when a lawyer messes up. In the X-ray example above, Phil also violated his duty to protect his client's property. Separate from the malpractice claim, you might have grounds for an ethics complaint to the state bar association. And an ethics violation may exist even if there was no malpractice. For example, most states' ethics rules prevent a lawyer from holding the client's file hostage. If a lawyer won't turn over the client's property until a client pays his bill in full, the client has an ethics complaint even if withholding the file doesn't rise to malpractice.

If you suspect your lawyer has committed malpractice or an ethics violation exists, consult with an attorney whose practice focuses on lawyer malpractice claims.

Ending the Relationship

A client may always fire his attorney. This isn't always true the other way around. Lawyers can't end an attorney-client relationship when doing so might prejudice the client or its interests. Is the attorney working on a big deal that's scheduled to close in the next two weeks? Then it's likely that the attorney must finish work on that job before she can quit, since another attorney won't have enough time to learn the deal and complete it. Mostly though, this restriction applies in the context of litigation.

When a lawyer represents a client in litigation, the lawyer's obligations to the court are also affected if the lawyer quits the case. Getting out of a case in litigation requires the court's permission. In litigation, the prejudice to the client from the lawyer's quitting is often easy to see. In one case I had sent discovery (written requests for information) to the other side and hadn't received the responses. My opposing counsel asked the court's permission to quit because the client wasn't paying his bill. Okay, the lawyer didn't say that, but he did say in his request that the client had "failed to fulfill an obligation to the attorney and firm," which is lawyer-speak for a client who hasn't paid. Even though the client owed the lawyer a lot of money, the court didn't let him quit. Why? Because if the discovery wasn't responded to in a timely manner, then the client would face negative consequences such as bars on his ability to present certain evidence and a sanctions award for not responding. It was easy to see that quitting would result in harm to the client. The court required the discovery responses be completed before the lawyer could resign.

A lawyer quitting when there's no new counsel for the client may disrupt the court's trial schedule. If the request to quit is too close to the trial date, it is unlikely that the court will dismiss the lawyer without the client's consent. When the client is a company, the court may require the lawyer to stay in the case until a new lawyer is hired.

When your lawyer wants out of the representation for any reason, your interests are usually better served by finding a replacement counsel than hoping the court forces your lawyer to keep representing you. Breaking up with your attorney shouldn't be hard to do for either of you.

• •

When you're in business, you need to have a relationship with an attorney. Vet your attorney for competency and fit. Once you hire your attorney, make sure you tell her all the information that might affect the representation. If you aren't sure if the lawyer needs the information, tell her anyway, and let her make the call. Except in some very limited circumstances, what you tell your lawyer will remain confidential, so you lose nothing by telling her. Try to bear with us. Remember, we have other clients and responsibilities. Sometimes we won't be able to answer your calls or respond as quickly as you may like. If your lawyer is non-responsive after a reasonable period of time, it's probably a signal that you need to hire someone new. Don't hamstring your attorney by not giving her information or by placing unreasonable limits on what she can do. Remember, our goal is to protect you to the maximum extent allowed by the law. Just like any relationship, sometimes things don't work out. Whether you are ending the relationship or the attorney is, the transition should be handled in a way that minimizes any potential harm to the client.

CLOSING

egal landmines don't have to destroy your business. While every business will run into difficulties at times, and maybe even litigation, taking a proactive approach to the existing legal challenges helps minimize the damage caused when collision is unavoidable.

Remember the story of Raj, Maria and Bob I told you in the introduction? It's okay, I'll wait while you skim to remember which story that was … Back? Great. The company lost hundreds of thousands of dollars because it failed to plan ahead. It didn't have to be that way.

One company, Red Baron Co., sought my help in its start-up phase. The owners were two service-disabled veterans and a woman, we'll call her Heidi, whom they'd worked with for years after their retirement from the military. Heidi was to be the company's Chief Financial Officer and own ten percent of the company for working for essentially no pay during those start-up years. Like Raj, Maria and Bob's tech company, all owners were to work in the business. As I suggested in Chapter 5, and advised them, their shareholders' agreement had provisions that would allow a majority of the shareholders to fire another shareholder and buy back his stock if that shareholder wasn't performing, and for a host of other reasons. Over the years, the company grew and prospered and added two more shareholders. Each time a new owner joined the company, we amended the shareholder's agreement so everyone knew and agreed there were ways of firing them.

About *five years* into the business, the company started having some internal issues. Specifically, Heidi wasn't capable of performing her duties for a large company. She was submitting invoices late, which at times resulted in the company not getting paid for its work, and she wasn't projecting the cash flow to see when a crunch would happen. Over a six-month period, the other shareholders would scramble two or three days before payroll to obtain funds to loan the company to cover that payroll. Despite being required to loan her share of funds to the company in this situation, Heidi never loaned any money to help. Her continued failure to plan for these financial crunches remained after many meetings to educate her on what information was needed and when.

Eventually, the other four owners said, "Enough." It wasn't worth paying her a six-figure salary and ten percent of the profits when they were hiring staff to do her job and still couldn't get the financial information the company needed. The other owners implemented the buy-out provision in the shareholders' agreement, fired Heidi as an employee and transferred her stock to the company. Heidi still had the right to be paid for her stock ownership, but because she'd been fired for cause, she was only owed ten dollars. Now, the company offered to pay her severance pay, to pay her insurance premiums for six months, and to pay a premium on her stock repurchase in return for a release of claims because the offer would be less expensive for the company than fighting with her.

Heidi was, understandably, upset. She hired an attorney who alleged a whole bunch of silly things, such as that Heidi had been fired solely because she was female while the rest of the owners were male and that the company had manufactured cause when she'd been doing an extraordinary job in her position. And the financial crunches weren't Heidi's fault. Well, there was some truth to that last part. The company knew a year in advance that because of how the billing cycle worked on government contracts, there would be a window when cash flow would likely be negative and all shareholders would need to loan the business money. This is why Heidi's ability to forecast the company's cash flow needs was critical. She simply didn't have the skills to do so. And Heidi made the problem worse by failing to bill other contracts or billing late, which resulted in the company losing over forty thousand dollars for work performed. The financial bump became a fissure.

The company responded with its documented employment file, showing when the issues had been raised and corrective plans put into place, the shareholders' agreement and the documents showing the agreement's buyback terms had been complied with. The additional legal expense to repel the later claim was under five thousand dollars.

It bears repeating. Proactively handling potential employ-ment and legal issues cost Red Baron only five thousand dollars. But failing to take similar steps cost Raj and Maria's company hundreds of thousands of dollars in losses and legal expense in their dispute with Maria. While some legal problems can be fixed after you hit a legal landmine, the price to do so is always dramatically higher.

Fear and dread, what I call drag, kill the joy and the dream. But now you have the strongest weapon you can wield against them. You know the saying "knowledge is power"? Well, now that power belongs to you.

This book has given you the tools to identify and avoid the most common legal landmines that entrepreneurs and business owners stumble over. You have a deeper understanding of some of the more common legal provisions and the risks embedded in them. In turn, this understanding allows you to better protect your business and your dream from costly mistakes. Walk confidently in your business, knowing that when the drag of life comes you've robbed it of its ability to be stronger than your desires and dreams.

By using the tips in this book, you can build a strong legal foundation for your business, your employees and your life. There is no need to feel intimidated by others who have been in business longer, or made more money. You are playing on the same level field. More than that, you don't have to go it alone. You have the resources you need to interview and find the right legal professional.

Life can bring us to our knees, but it's also waiting for us to say, "I'm ready!" and then to unveil the gifts it has for us. It's time for your perfect day riding in the summer sun.

Are you ready?

RESOURCES

The book may be over, but I'd never leave you without resources.

For more tips, please check out my website and blog at:
AttorneyNancyGreene.com

My YouTube Channel at:
youtube.com/channel/UCfWnr3woqTWfxA4v-blmpZg

Facebook page at:
facebook.com/attorneynancygreene/

Twitter at:
@attynancygreene

If you are interested in my business consulting services, including business evaluations and training, please check out:

My website at:
AttorneyNancyGreene.com

Email me at:
Nancy@AttorneyNancyGreene.com

Or call me at:
(703) 836-1000

NANCY D. GREENE, ESQUIRE

If you are interested in my legal services, please contact me:

My website at:
AttorneyNancyGreene.com

Email me at:
Ngreene@landcarroll.com

Or call me at:
(703) 836-1000.

GLOSSARY

Ambiguous – Having one or more possible meanings. If a contract provision is ambiguous it is unlikely to be enforced by the court.

Associate – A junior attorney in a law firm. Generally, an attorney with seven or fewer years of experience.

Attorney-client privilege – This doctrine generally prevents disclosure of the information a client tells his attorney where that communication is made in confidence within the attorney-client relationship for the purpose of seeking, obtaining or providing legal advice or assistance to the client or potential client. The privilege is not absolute and can be waived by the client when the client seeks to use the lawyer's advice to commit a fraud or another criminal act and for the lawyer to defend himself in actions with the client.

At will – In relation to an employee's term of employment, this means the employee can be fired at any time for any reason, so long as it's not an illegal reason, with or without notice. The opposite is *term* employment, where the employee is guaranteed work for a specific period of time and can generally only be fired when that time period ends or if certain predetermined events occur.

Boilerplate provision – A standardized clause or provision in a contract. These provisions aren't content-specific, meaning that the provision will appear in different types of documents without modification.

Breach of contract – A cause of action where one side has not fully performed its obligations under a contract. To establish a claim, the plaintiff must prove there was a contract, the other side failed to complete or perform a material part of the agreement and the plaintiff was damaged, usually in the form of a monetary loss, as a result of the breach.

Buy-sell agreement – A binding contract between owners of a business that sets out the conditions and terms when one owner may or must purchase the other owner's interest in the company.

Common law – The laws of the land that are determined by custom or the courts (judicial precedent) rather than by a statute passed by some legislative entity.

Confidential information – Generally, this is information that an individual or business wishes to keep secret or limited to a specific group of people and is related to trade secrets, processes, business operations, works or any other information related to a business's operations that might be sensitive or give a competitor an advantage if known to them.

Conflict of interest – A situation where the impartiality of the lawyer may be undermined because of conflicting duties to multiple clients or former clients or their own interests.

Consumer – A person who buys goods or services for primarily personal, family or household use. As an example, buying a computer for your child is a consumer purchase while buying the same computer for the office would not be a consumer transaction.

Consumer protection laws – State laws designed to protect a consumer in consumer transactions from unfair business practices such as fraud and unfair or deceptive practices. Significant penalties exist for businesses that violate these laws.

Contingent fee – A billing agreement between an attorney and a client where the attorney agrees to accept a set percentage of the amount paid to the client as a result of the case in satisfaction of his legal fees. If the case is not successful, the lawyer will not receive any compensation for fees, but may be entitled to payment of his hard costs, like filing fees and court reporter fees.

Discovery – The process in litigation where each side can obtain evidence in the form of written answers to questions, production of documents and sworn testimony from the other parties to the dispute and from individuals who might have knowledge about the matter. Generally, the process includes interrogatories (sworn written answers to questions), production of documents responsive to specific requests, requests for admissions of certain facts, depositions (sworn verbal testimony under oath) and subpoenas (requests for documents from individuals not directly involved in the lawsuit when those documents relate to the subject matter of the suit).

Estate – The property or possessions, including legal claims and other intangible rights, belonging to a person. In a bankruptcy context, this term is broadly defined to relate to any rights belonging to the debtor (the person filing bankruptcy). The term estate is also used with regard to the property and rights of a deceased person.

Executor/executrix – The person or company appointed by an individual in his will or by the court to carry out the terms of the will and administer that person's estate after his death.

Fruit of the poisonous tree – This is a criminal law concept that prevents the prosecutor from using evidence that was illegally obtained, and anything traceable to the illegally obtained information, against the defendant.

Heirs – The people or companies entitled to receive any portion of an estate on a person's death.

Indemnify/indemnification clause – Protects a person or company from certain kinds of expenses, damages, losses or claims in the future in case certain events occur.

Injunction – An order of the court that either requires someone to take a specific action or stop taking a specific action. These orders can be temporary until trial or permanent, usually granted after trial. Generally, to obtain an injunction a party seeking the court's assistance must show: They are likely to win the case; there will be irreparable harm (meaning damages that money alone won't fix) if there is no injunction; the harm to the other side will be outweighed by the benefit to the party getting the injunction; and the public in general wouldn't be harmed by the entry of an injunction.

Malpractice – Literally this term means "bad practice." It is a failure of a professional duty or the exercise of ordinary care and skill in performing professional services which results in injury, loss or damage. To establish legal malpractice, the former client will often have to show that, but for the lawyer's mistake, the client would have won or not been damaged.

Master-servant relationship – This is an archaic term referring to the legal relationship between an employer (the master) and its employee (the servant) whereby the employer can be held legally responsible for the acts of its employee.

Motion – A request for action from a judge on a particular matter in a case. Most motions must be in writing and set out the legal basis for the court to take the requested action.

Negligence – Failure to adhere to a standard of care or duty of care owed to an individual that causes harm to that person.

Non-circumvention agreement/provision – A contract or term in a contract where parties to a business deal agree only to use the other party's information or contacts for the purposes of the business relationship between the two parties and not to benefit from the information without sharing that benefit with the business partner.

Non-competition agreement – A contract or term in a contract that restricts an individual, usually a former employee, from certain actions after the relationship with the previous employer has ended.

Partner – A person who takes part in an undertaking with another or others, especially in a business or company with shared risks and profits. Partnerships do not have the protection of the corporate shield and the individual partners are personally responsible for company debt. Colloquially, this term also means any individual with whom you are in business whether they be partners, shareholders, members or another company pursuing a joint goal with your business. In the law firm context, this term usually refers to a senior attorney at a firm. A law partner may be a shareholder or member in the firm or have no equity interest.

Prejudice – A fact or condition which, if proven by a party to the litigation, may defeat the other side's claim. Cases are dismissed (ended) with prejudice once they have been finally ruled on.

Pro bono – Legal representation for "the public good" where the lawyer agrees to represent a party (usually the plaintiff) in litigation without payment from the client in order to vindicate some public right.

Restrictive covenant – These provisions are essentially voluntary injunctions agreed to by the parties to the contract. A restrictive covenant is a term that requires a party to do or not do something based on certain conditions. When applied in the employment context, it generally prevents former employees from competing with their former employer or offering competing services to that company's customers.

Subtenant – A person who rents real property from another tenant rather than directly from the landlord.

Trade Secret – This term is generally defined by state law under each state's version of the Uniform Trade Secrets Act. Generally, a trade secret is any practice or process of a company that has commercial value and isn't known outside the company, and for which the company has taken reasonable steps to keep secret. Examples include formulas, programs, devices, methods, techniques or processes. Not all confidential information qualifies as a trade secret.

Unfair prejudice or *prejudice* – All evidence is prejudicial to someone's case or claim but sometimes the risk of harm from the evidence is greater than its ability to reveal the truth. Evidence is unfairly prejudicial when it refers to information that would suggest a decision on an improper basis.

APPENDIX A

Statute of Limitations Chart**

** This chart is a guide and for informational purposes. You should not rely on this chart to determine the time limits for your claim. Always check your state's actual statutes of limitation for the time limit for your specific claim, which may differ from what you read here. Also, some states have different statutes of limitations for promissory notes and open-ended accounts including credit card debts. These limitations may be longer or shorter than those set out here. Certain types of breaches of contracts may have different time periods. The time period set forth below is in years.

State	Statute	Written Contract	Oral Contract
Alabama	Ala. Code § 6-2-30, et seq.	6	6
Alaska	Alaska Stat. §09.10.010	3	3
Arizona	Ariz. Rev. Stat. Ann. §12-541, et seq.	6	3
Arkansas	Ark. Code Ann. §16-56-101, et seq.	5	3
California	Cal. Civ. Proc. Code §312, et seq.	4	2
Colorado	Colo. Rev. Stat. §13-80-101, et seq.	3 (6 most debts/ rent) (2 for tortious breach)	3 (6 short-term debts/ rent) (2 for tortious breach)

State	Statute		
Connecticut	Conn. Gen. Stat. Ann. §52-575, et seq.	6	3
Delaware	Del. Code. Ann. Tit. 10 §8101, et seq.	3	3
D.C.	DC Code §12-301, et seq.	3	3
Florida	Fla. Stat. Ann. §95.011, et seq.	4	4
Georgia	Ga. Code Ann. §9-3-20, et seq.	6	4
Hawaii	Haw. Rev. Stat. §657-1, et seq.	6	6
Idaho	Idaho Code §5-201, et seq.	5	4
Illinois	735 Ill. Comp. Stat. 5/13-201, et seq.	10	5
Indiana	Ind. Code Ann. §34-11-2-1, et seq.	10	6
Iowa	Iowa Code Ann. §614.1, et seq.	10	5
Kansas	Kan. Stat. Ann. §60-501, et seq.	5	3
Kentucky	Ky. Rev. Stat. Ann. §413.080, et seq.	10 (15 years for contracts before July 15, 2014	5
Louisiana	La. Civil Code §3492, et seq.	10	10
Maine	Me. Rev. Stat. Ann Tit. 14 § 751, et seq.	6	6
Maryland	Md. Courts & Jud. Proc. Code Ann. §5-101, et seq.	3	3
Massachusetts	Mass. Ann. Laws Ch. 260 §1, et seq.	6	6
Michigan	Mich. Comp. Laws §600.5801, et seq.	6	6
Minnesota	Minn. Stat. Ann. §541.01, et seq.	6	6
Mississippi	Miss. Code. Ann. §15-1-1, et seq.	6	3
Missouri	Mo. Rev. Stat. §516.097, et. seq.	10 (some cases only 5)	5
Montana	Mont. Code Ann. §27-2-202, et seq.	8	5
Nebraska	Neb. Rev. Stat. §24-201, et seq.	5	4
Nevada	Nev. Rev. Stat. Ann. §11.010 et seq.	6	4
New Hampshire	NH Rev. Stat. Ann. §508.1, et seq.	3	3
New Jersey	NJ Stat. Ann. §2a:14-1, et seq.	6	6
New Mexico	NM Stat. Ann.§37-1-1, et seq.	6	4
New York	NY Civ. Prac. Laws & Rules §201, et seq.	6	6
North Carolina	NC Gen. Stat §1-46, et seq.	3	3
North Dakota	ND Cent. Code §28-01-01, et seq.	6	6
Ohio	Ohio Rev. Code Ann. §2305.03, et seq.	8	6
Oklahoma	Okla. Stat. Ann. Tit 12 §91, et seq.	5	3
Oregon	Or. Rev. Stat §12.010, et seq.	6	6
Pennsylvania	42 Pa. Cons. Stat. Ann. §5501, et seq.	4	4

Rhode Island	RI Gen. Laws §9-1-12, et seq.	10	10
South Carolina	SC Code Ann. §15-3-510, et seq.	3	3
South Dakota	SD Codified Laws Ann. §15-2-1, et seq.	6	6
Tennessee	Tenn. Code Ann. §28-3-101, et seq.	6	6
Texas	Tex. Civ. Prac. & Rem. Code §16.001, et seq. Tex. Bus. & Com. Code Ann. §2.725	4	4
Utah	Utah Code Ann. §78B-2-101, et seq.	6	4
Vermont	Vt. Stat. Ann. Tit 12 §461, et seq.	6	6
Virginia	Va. Code Ann.§8.01-228, et seq.	5	3
Washington	Wash. Rev. Code Ann. §4.16.005, et seq.	6	3
West Virginia	W. VA Code §55-2-1, et seq.	10	5
Wisconsin	Wis. Stat. Ann. §893.01, et seq.	6	6
Wyoming	Wyo. State §1-3-102, et seq.	10	8

ABOUT THE AUTHOR

After twenty years as a business lawyer and litigator and tired of the heartbreak of business owners losing everything from avoidable mistakes, Nancy's mission is to inspire, educate, and empower business owners. In this DIY society there are very limited legal resources for small to mid-sized businesses. It became her mission to demystify all that fancy legal-mumbo jumbo and help businesses leverage the law. She's developed a series of YouTube Videos and blog posts about avoiding some of the most common legal landmines for your business and has a new podcast starting in March, 2017, to assist business owners avoid the Legal Landmines that can destroy their businesses.

Starting her own law firm in 2013, Nancy understands business. In April, 2016, Nancy joined Land, Carroll & Blair PC as a principal. Her practice focuses on business litigation, employment law, women-owned businesses, start-up business and those businesses in transition from family to legacy business.

A bestselling author, member of the National Association of Professional Women, NAPW Woman of the Year 2012/2013, and EWomen Network platinum member, when Nancy's not practicing law, she's spending time on her horse farm with her husband and two teenage boys, and writing fiction under her pen name Nancy DiMauro.

Be sure to read Nancy's other business help book *Succeeding Through Doubt, Fear and Crisis*.

www.ingramcontent.com/pod-product-compliance
Lightning Source LLC
Chambersburg PA
CBHW060356220326
41598CB00023B/2943